THE HOLY BIBLE: MUSLIM OBJECTIONS AND CHRISTIAN RESPONSES

Confirming the truth in the light of history, reason and inspiration

ABDUL RUB

Copyright © 2015 Abdul Rub
All rights reserved.
ISBN: 1507630190
ISBN-13:9781507630198

DEDICATION

I dedicate this book to the following persons:

1. My Lord and Saviour Jesus Christ who gave His life that we might live forever!
2. Faithful Christian Background Believers (CBBs) such as NMM Bhakthraj who remain faithful to the Lord Jesus Christ till the end. When I was a young believer, brother Bhakthraj was a living example of humility and love. In the latter part of his life, although he was surrounded by the Islamic *dawah* preachers, he remained faithful to his Saviour Jesus Christ till the end. As a matter of fact, the final words lingered on his lips just before he stepped into glory were the repetition of the saving name of 'Jesus!'
3. Courageous Muslim Background Believers (MBBs) such as Sultan, my long term associate, who pay heavy price to embrace Christ. When Sultan was a teenager, he found the truth that caused him to leave Islam and embrace Christ. The result of that was swift and severe. His own father and mother tried to harm him for the decision he had made. The Lord intervened and protected him. Sultan survived till today as a testimony of God's faithfulness. For more than three decades Sultan has been on the run from his own people who sought his life. There are countless MBBs who dare to take a similar path to that of Sultan's.
4. My God-given wife and two children who paid dearly to enable me to put this book together for God's glory.

ACKNOWLEDGEMENTS

I would like to express my deep appreciation to my wife and Bro. Chacko who motivated and encouraged me to start as well as finish this book. I am also thankful to Bro. Rod who has done the editing work in order to see this book in this form.

CONTENTS

Preface..7

Introduction..9

    1. The Holy Bible: The Only True Word of God..............15

    2. Muslims' Understanding of the Word of God..............43

    3. Problems with Muslims' Position............................57

    4. Christian Position on the Qur'an............................67

    5. Muslim Questions and Christian Answers................105

    6. Some Exegetical Principles..................................203

Bibliography..208

PREFACE

Is the Bible a compilation of mere human accounts or is it God's word for mankind given in human languages under divine inspiration?
Is the Bible filled with contradictions and errors or is it only a case of the Bible being misunderstood and misrepresented!
Does the Bible teach irrational doctrines or is it because the Bible is too lofty for the human mind to comprehend?

These are some of the questions that crop up and create barriers between Muslims and Christians when it comes to discussing the Bible.

This book is the result of much prayerful consideration after meeting many Christians, particularly in India, who asked for resources to answer the Muslim questions raised against the Bible. For most Christians that the Bible is God's word is a given. It was never debated, discussed or even thought about. That is why today's average Christian can be easily lured into a battle field that is totally unfamiliar; he or she struggles even to just hold on to the ground, let alone fight the challengers.

Owing to this situation, it is becoming increasingly common for Muslims to challenge Christians regarding the authenticity as well as reliability of the Bible in an effort to destroy the very foundation of the Christian faith so that the unsuspecting Christian can be easily led away from light into darkness. This situation is impelling some Christians to look for solutions and resources to enable them face the challenge. Through this little effort I am trying to meet that need in some very practical ways.

Christian faith is characterized by threefold-truths that provide spiritual tenacity to the true believer for *'a cord of three strands is not quickly broken'* (Eccl.4:12). At its core lay three fundamental beliefs, namely, belief in the One true God who is triune, and belief in His word the Holy Bible, and belief in the salvation that is available only in the person of Jesus Christ and what He has done.

This book is devoted to highlight the reliability and authenticity of the second core belief of the Christian faith i.e. the Bible is God's word, in the face of Muslim apologists' relentless attacks on it.

The major purpose of this book is twofold. One, to provide helpful responses to the objections and questions raised by our Muslim friends against the Bible due to their misunderstanding of the holy Scriptures. Two, to help Christians get equipped in the truth of the Bible in order for them to be able to lift up God's word high enough that it may draw people unto the Saviour. However, this book is not a manual that explains how to share the gospel with Muslims nor is it intended to provide information to attack Muslims and malign their faith. Therefore, readers must take utmost care in dealing with the information given in this book. As far as the sharing of the gospel is concerned we Christians must share the gospel with love and in a non-offensive way (Eph.4:15).

In this book, I am focusing on highlighting as well as addressing some of the enigmas, misconceptions and misinterpretations of the Bible which is the foundation of the Christian faith. More than seventy such instances related to the Bible have been dealt with for the benefit of the believers as well as non-believers.

As the author of this book I admit that the answers and responses presented in this book are in no way the best or the only possible responses to the objections it addresses. This book is primarily intended to prepare Christians in their belief about the Bible as well as Muslim's belief in the Quran even before they get engaged in practical interactions and meaningful dialogues with Muslim friends about the gospel.

If you find any factual errors in the contents of this book or could not find help in a particular issue that is of grave concern to you within the scope of this book, we request you to write to us with the relevant information or queries so that we can do our best to address them in the next edition of this book.

All glory, honor and praise be to the true God—the Father, the Son and the Holy Spirit!

In the service of the Lord,
Abdul Rub
<Abdulrub4god@gmail.com>

INTRODUCTION

God exists. He is the Creator of all that came into existence. He is not a mere static energy or force, but a personal Being with the ability to communicate. God created mankind in His own image and likeness, and enabled it to commune and communicate with Him. The way God communicated with mankind in human history was chiefly through His word that was revealed to chosen individuals. Intended for all times, this was committed to written forms under divine inspiration and is known as the scriptures (cf. Isaiah 30:8). The collection of these scriptures into one volume is called the Holy Bible. And as God purposed, the Bible has been passed down faithfully through many generations.

Ever since God began to reveal His word - the Holy Bible - some three and a half thousand years ago, it has faced many objections and attacks. The unbelievers in this world have not only been rejecting and mocking God's word but have also been trying their best to destroy the indestructible word of God through their futile arguments and efforts. However, God being sovereign, has declared, "My word abides forever" (Isaiah 40:8 & 1Peter 1:25).

In addition to its theoretical as well as theological soundness, the Holy Bible exerts a tremendous authority over those who believe in it providing them supernatural transformation in their lives and attitudes that confirms its divine origin.

There are countless individuals like Ishmael who made a complete about-turn in his attitude towards the Holy Bible when he encountered its message and power. I met brother Ishmael in the year 2014, and had the privilege of staying with his simple and god-fearing family. He comes from a traditional Muslim family.

When he was young, his parents became followers of Jesus Christ and embraced Christianity; this shook their relatives and the whole Muslim community in their locality.

This unexpected change of religious beliefs of his parents troubled young Ishmael and provoked him to expose the 'falsity' of the Bible for everyone to see.

With this one single purpose in mind, Ishmael enrolled himself in a Bible school. By the end of the first year, his passionate and ardent efforts to disprove the Bible as God's word had the opposite effect on him. At the end of his second year, Ishmael finished studying the Bible as a devout 'born-again' believer! Today, God is using Ishmael as an effective tool in His hands to bring other Muslims to the living Saviour Jesus Christ, through the message of the Holy Bible. I've met several former Muslims with similar testimonies.

However, the enemy of God the devil who is also called Satan has been tirelessly working through some individuals and institutions to make false accusations and allegations against God and His word in order to mislead people and turn them away from the truth of God. It is sad but alarmingly true that many sincere people have unwittingly fallen prey to these efforts of the evil one and are in danger of losing God's precious blessings for all eternity. May God protect the reader of this book from such perils!

Over the centuries, Muslim enthusiasts have been framing innumerable questions and objections against the Holy Bible based on their Islam-conditioned understanding of who God is and what His word is like. Some of them are overtly bent on doing this in order to malign the Christian faith that the Bible is God's word.

In these modern days, Muslim apologists such as Ahmed Deedat from South Africa, Shabir Ally from Canada, Zakir Naik from India, and several other mushrooming Muslim apologists around the world who try to imitate these so-called Islamic stalwarts, have gone to great lengths in framing fallacious and outrageous arguments against the Bible, crossing borders of all rationality, honesty and civility. It is Ahmad Deedat who spearheaded the vicious attacks on the authenticity as well as the contents of the Bible in the past four decades. In his efforts Deedat employed fallacious arguments, deception and hypocrisy to malign God's word. In addition to preaching and debating in a number of western countries against the Bible, Deedat also wrote quite a number of books spewing his venomous declarations against God's holy word.

In the end Deedat paid heavily for his arrogance and blasphemies. On April 6, 1996 in Sydney, Australia he made highly offensive comments against the Holy Bible and the crucifixion and resurrection of the Lord Jesus Christ. Four week later, on May 3rd he was stricken by a rare kind of stroke that paralyzed him for the rest of his life. He lost his speech and was bedridden till his death that took place on August 8, 2005.

Along with Deedat's all the other major Muslim apologists' fallacious arguments have been refuted thoroughly and appropriately, and their hypocrisy is exposed for all to see at the world's best Christian apologetic website dealing with Muslim polemics:
http://answering-islam.org/Responses/index.htm

Interestingly, in spite of the dishonest and evil campaigns directed against the Holy Bible many pious Muslims who are hungry for truth and salvation are coming to Christ all over the world in large numbers just by studying the Bible with open minds and hearts.

For the past one year I have been worshipping at a church that has around a hundred members. More than ninety percent of the members, including the pastor, were once Muslims. Almost all of them left Islam for Christ within the past twenty five years. It is a vibrant witnessing church reaching out to other Muslims with the Gospel. I am thankful to God for giving me the privilege to be a part of it.

If you are a committed follower of Christ, it is incumbent upon you that you be a witness of Christ to the world, and that world includes Muslims. The minimum responsibility on you to be a witness for Christ is to have an unshakeable faith in His word i.e. the Holy Bible. I highly recommend that you keep on reading the Holy Bible regularly and from the beginning to the end so that you can complete the whole Bible not just once in your lifetime but as many times as your lifespan allows. This particular spiritual discipline is so vital for fortifying your stand in God through Christ, with the help of the Holy Spirit.

Several years ago I heard the testimony of an old man who read the whole Bible for more than forty times! This has encouraged me to commit myself to reading the Bible continuously for the rest of my life. As I am writing this, I am reading through the book of Psalms in an effort to read the Bible through for the twelfth time! To be sure, our salvation and God's grace toward us do not depend on how many times we read the Bible, but this act does reflect our attitude towards God's word and the place we give it in our lives.

Let's remember C.S. Lewis' well known saying about the Bible and sin, 'Either the Bible will keep you away from sin, or sin will keep you away from the Bible.' This way you can make your spiritual foundation secure and at the same time help others as well to have the same strong spiritual foundation.

In addition to reading the whole Bible, I would also like to encourage you to read the whole Qur'an at least once. Many years ago I lived in the capital city of a Muslim dominated country. During my interactions with local Muslims I heard from quite a number of Muslims that I continued as a Christian because I had never read the Qur'an. They told me that had I read the Qur'an, I would have known the truth and that would have made me a Muslim!

Of course, I turned the tables on them by pointing out to them about their failure to know the truth of the Holy Bible for the same reason. Despite following this line of counter argument on the spur of the moment, later I took it as a challenge and finished reading the whole Qur'an in about a month. This exercise gave me a tremendous leverage over Muslims in my subsequent interactions with them. It provided me more opportunities to talk with Muslims and I was able to often get unhindered attention from my Muslim listeners while I was sharing what I always wanted to share with them.

Religious discussions with Muslims would often prompt them to attack the Bible that is the foundation for our spiritual life. Therefore, it is imperative on our part to be aware of what kind of questions they use in their attack on the Bible and how to respond to them in a way that would bring glory to God and blessings to those Muslims too.

Before we address the common and significant questions Muslims raise against God's word, let's first understand what the Bible is, why it is reliable, how it is different from other religious books and what it offers which other books cannot.

> Hate those who love you
> (*Devil's teaching*)
> Hate those who hate you and love those who love you
> (*Moral teaching*)
> Love even those who hate and persecute you
> (*Divine teaching*)

1. THE HOLY BIBLE: THE ONLY TRUE WORD OF GOD

In the recent past the religious world has witnessed the murder of many a literary scholar and critique in the hands of religious fanatics whose goal is to keep certain religious books out of critical analysis in their determination to perpetuate blind faith in them at all cost.

In contrast, history also offers a number of examples that show us how some godly men and women embraced death in its cruelest form in order to make the Bible accessible to common people and critiques alike, in their own languages.

As a result, the message of the Bible has been translated into more than 2800 languages of the world as of 2013. Of these 513 languages have the complete Bible (Old Testament and New Testament); nearly 1300 languages have the whole New Testament and another 1000 languages have at least one book of the Bible. The Bible continues to be the most translated, distributed, and read book in the history of mankind! No other book comes anywhere near to this achievement. It is God, as its author, who made this giant achievement a reality.

The Bible has demonstrated its incredible supernatural power in many different ways. One of the delightful and awe-inspiring testimonies that affirm this fact to me is the story of Yesudas. I have known Yesudas and his wife since 1986, the year I was saved by the grace of God into His kingdom.

My friend Yesudas, having grown up illiterate in a remote village in south India, heard the gospel and came to worship the one true God, abandoning his previous devotion to Hindu deities. As he began to pray for friends and family members, Yesudas regretted that he could not read in order to know and understand the Bible better. One afternoon at the cotton factory where he worked, Yesudas prayed about this problem. He heard a distinct voice telling him to read Luke chapter 12, verse 12. The voice persisted for about fifteen minutes. At home that evening, Yesudas immediately searched for a Bible his brother had left in their home. When he found it, he opened it and read—not only verse 12, but all of Luke 12. His wife was stupefied at the sight of her illiterate husband reading the Bible. Since that day, Yesudas reads and writes in his mother tongue. All who knew him were filled with joy and encouragement in their faith. Today Yesudas and his wife are church-planters, trusting in the power of God's Word at work in and through their lives.

There are countless individuals in our generation whose lives have been transformed by the power of the Holy Bible. Their transformation may not be as dramatic as that of Yesudas but each transformation is inexplicable if you fail to reckon the hand of God in them.

The Bible is the collection of several divinely inspired books of God. These individual books were faithfully passed down through generations. In the subsequent generations these books were again identified, authenticated and separated from other ancient literature under stringent evaluation processes. The sixty-six canonical books from both Jewish and Christian Scriptures, that were in circulation among the believing communities in scattered forms, were finally re-affirmed, re-confirmed and grouped together in one volume called the Holy Bible toward the end of the fourth century.

THE ONLY TRUE WORD OF GOD

The English word 'Bible' derived through the Latin word *Biblia* which itself was derived through the Greek *ta Biblia* meaning 'the Books.' The singular form of this Greek word is *Biblion*, whose meaning is book or scroll. The Greek word *Biblion* from which the English word 'Bible' is derived has been used in the Greek manuscripts of the O.T. (*Septuagint*: Dan.9:2) and also N.T. (Lk.4:17-20; Jn.20:30; Acts 1:20; Gal.3:10; Rev.22:18-19) to refer to the 'books' given by God i.e. the Holy Bible.

The Bible that contains thirty-nine Jewish Scriptures and twenty-seven Christian Scriptures together is the divinely inspired word of God to mankind. Any book outside of these sixty-six inspired books is to be treated as mere human production.

The Bible is not a compilation of the ancient literature penned by mere human authors. It's not a book that can be analyzed with academic skills or can be understood by intellectual prowess. Rather it's the body of the divine revelations in recorded form that need to be discerned and deciphered under *illuminating* power of God.

The overall revelation of God to mankind had been progressive. The Jewish Scriptures – *Tanakh* as Jews call or the Old Testament as Christians call – are the first and the basic revelation of God, whereas the Christians Scriptures or the New Testament is the final and finished revelation of God to mankind. Together they form the whole revelation of God to mankind. It is the New Testament that completes, interprets and authenticates the Old Testament (Tanakh). Yet, both Testaments are from the same one true God. That is why Christians not only declare that they believe in both books as God's word, but also put them together and study them both for the spiritual edification and enlightenment.

The time and context specific 'laws of religion' prescribed in the Old Testament are binding only on Jewish nation up until the Messiah's first coming. But the 'laws of grace' prescribed in the New Testament are for all peoples and for all times.

"All Scripture is God-breathed and is useful for teaching, rebuking, correcting and training in righteousness, so that the servant of God may be thoroughly equipped for every good work." (1Tim.3:16-17)
"Above all, you must understand that no prophecy of Scripture came about by the prophet's own interpretation of things. For prophecy never had its origin in the human will, but prophets, though human, spoke from God as they were carried along by the Holy Spirit." (2Pet.1:20-21)

All Scripture – Jewish Scripture (Old Testament) and Christian Scripture (New Testament) – is God-breathed or inspired. All of it is useful for teaching, rebuking, correcting and training in righteousness. Some accounts in the Scripture are given as positive examples to follow and others are recorded to serve as warnings or negative examples to shun evil. Whatever is immoral according to the Old Testament is also immoral according to the New Testament. But, whatever the Old Testament prescribes may not necessarily be applicable according to the New Testament unless it is prescribed in it.

The 'Chicago Statement on Biblical Inerrancy' was produced at an international Summit Conference of evangelical leaders in 1978. In its Article VI it affirms "that the whole of Scripture and all its parts, down to the very words of the original, were given by divine inspiration." And in its Article X it affirms "that inspiration, strictly speaking, applies only to the autographic text of Scripture, which in the providence of God can be ascertained from available manuscripts with great accuracy. We further affirm that copies and translations of Scripture are the Word of God to the extent that they faithfully represent the original." (http://www.bible-researcher.com/chicago1.html)

Basic understanding of a few important terms and concepts that belong to the Christian faith with regard to the Bible is the first step toward forming a proper view of the Holy Bible. Below we see some Christian terms that need to be understood properly before we move further in our journey to understand the believers view on the Bible.

Revelation: It is God given intuition or understanding or knowledge or experience. This can come in the form of dreams or visions or sudden knowledge. God in His sovereignty can give this to anybody He chooses.

Inspiration: It is the divine superintendence or guidance undertaken by the Holy Spirit. This can result in supernatural actions or declarations or recording of the scriptures or receiving revelations from God. God in his sovereignty granted this divine inspiration to prophets, priests, rulers, apostles and evangelists at various times and places in the past.

Scriptures: The records made under inspiration are called Scriptures. The Scriptures were recorded in two ways. One, simultaneous inspiration—they were recorded by the inspired persons or their scribes as the Holy Spirit guided them. Two, stage-wise inspiration—some of these records have had inspiration at two stages.

In the first stage the revelations were received under inspiration. In the second stage the revelations that had been received under inspiration, were recorded again under inspiration. These Scriptures are called 'God's word or word of God to mankind.' They are given in human languages through human agencies, but under God's inspiration. The giving of these scriptures was active only during the prophetic and apostolic ages - not anymore.

GOD'S WORD

The Bible is God's word, not because it is written down personally by God or dictated by God or a spirit or an angel from God. The Bible is the 'word of God' because it is the written record of God's revelations under God's inspiration. Divine revelations were given to men of God, both naturally and supernaturally; and the men of God wrote them down for future generations under the superintendence or inspiration of God's Spirit.

The divine inspiration did not control or overrule, but made use of the natural talents and abilities of the men of God it stirred. In other words, the Bible is written by men, but inspired by God!

CONTENTS OF THE BIBLE

The Bible reveals the name, nature and plan of the Creator. It recounts the creation of mankind, states God's purpose for it and narrates the story of its fall. Finally, it describes the manifestation of the love of God that provided the way of salvation to sinful mankind.

GENRES OF THE BIBLE

God used several literary genres in His word. It has Law, History, Wisdom, Poetry, Romance, Gospel, Parables, Epistles, Prophecy, and Apocalyptic Literature.

LITERARY TECHNIQUES OF THE BIBLE

God, the author of the Bible, also used many literary techniques in His word. Some of the literary techniques we see in the Bible are paradox, imagery, hyperbole, satire, irony, symbolism, metaphor, anthropomorphism, first-person narration, second-person narration, third-person narration etc.

PURPOSE OF THE BIBLE

The Bible reveals who God is, what His will is and describes His interaction with His creation.

PROLIFERATION OF THE BIBLE

The Bible is the divine revelation to all peoples of all races, genders and languages in the world. It can be translated sufficiently into any language of the world without diminishing its truth or power proving that its author must be the Creator of all languages.

In the past 200 years (1816-2014) nearly 7 billion Bibles have been printed and sold or distributed worldwide. This took place despite the fact that many Muslim nations have banned the Bible from entering into their countries fearing the dominance of its truth and power against their state-sponsored religion. Now 100 million copies of the Bible are being printed annually. The Bible is by far the number one best-selling book and the most widely read book of all times!

INFLUENCE OF THE BIBLE

Our world has no shortage of the books that can influence and motivate their readers to kill others or even kill themselves for the sake of the deities and religions they promote. As a breath of fresh air through its message of love and forgiveness that was demonstrated through the life and mission of the final prophet – Saviour and Messiah - the Lord Jesus, the Bible has been transforming countless lives all over the world for better.

Those who have been thus transformed have time and again demonstrated the love of God in forgiving even their worst enemies. This is one of the fundamental qualities of the citizens of the kingdom of the true God. No other book or religion can come anywhere close to exerting this kind of influence and bringing about such a transformation in sinful human beings.

In the final analysis, it is God's sovereign will that oversaw the choosing of the languages, literary styles, content details and intended effects of His word given to mankind in the form of the Holy Bible.

> *Holy Bible: Jewish Scriptures—39 books &*
> *Christian Scriptures—27 books*

NAMES OF THE INDIVIDUAL BOOKS OF THE HOLY BIBLE, THEIR WRITERS AND APPROXIMATE DATES OF THEIR WRITING:

Old Testament

Book	Inspired Writer	Date Written
Genesis	Moses	around 1445 B.C.
Exodus	Moses	1445 - 1405 B.C.
Leviticus	Moses	around 1405 B.C.
Numbers	Moses	1444 - 1405 B.C.
Deuteronomy	Moses	around 1405 B.C.
Joshua	Joshua	1404-1390 B.C.
Judges	Samuel	1374-1129 B.C.
Ruth	Samuel	around 1150 B.C.
First Samuel	Samuel	1043-1011 B.C.
Second Samuel	Ezra*	1011-1004 B.C.
First Kings	Jeremiah*	971-852 B.C.
Second Kings	Jeremiah*	852-587 B.C.
First Chronicles	Ezra*	450 - 425 B.C.
Second Chronicles	Ezra*	450 - 425 B.C.
Ezra	Ezra	538-520 B.C.
Nehemiah	Nehemiah	445 - 425 B.C.
Esther	Mordecai*	around 465 B.C.
Job	Solomon*	around 900 B.C.*
Psalms	David	around 1000 B.C.
Psalms	Sons of Korah: Psalms 42, 44-49, 84-85, 87; Asaph: Psalms 50, 73-83; Heman: Psalm 88; Ethan: Psalm 89; Hezekiah: Psalms 120-123, 128-130, 132, 134-136; Solomon: Psalms 72, 127.	
Proverbs	Solomon: 1-29 Agur: 30 Lemuel: 31	950 - 700 B.C.
Ecclesiastes	Solomon	around 935 B.C.
Song of Solomon	Solomon	around 965 B.C.

Isaiah	Isaiah	740 - 680 B.C.
Jeremiah	Jeremiah	627 - 585 B.C.
Lamentations	Jeremiah	around 586 B.C.
Ezekiel	Ezekiel	593-560 B.C.
Daniel	Daniel	605-536 B.C.
Hosea	Hosea	around 710 B.C.
Joel	Joel	around 835 B.C.
Amos	Amos	around 755 B.C.
Obadiah	Obadiah	840 or 586 B.C.
Jonah	Jonah	around 760 B.C.
Micah	Micah	around 700 B.C.
Nahum	Nahum	663 - 612 B.C.
Habakkuk	Habakkuk	around 607 B.C.
Zephaniah	Zephaniah	around 625 B.C.
Haggai	Haggai	around 520 B.C.
Zechariah	Zechariah	520 - 518 B.C.
Malachi	Malachi	450 - 600 B.C.

New Testament

Book	Inspired Writer	Date Written (A.D)
Matthew	Matthew	in 60s
Mark	John Mark	late 50s early 60s
Luke	Luke	around 60
John	John	late 80s early 90s
Acts	Luke	around 61
Romans	Paul	around 55
1 Corinthians	Paul	around 54
2 Corinthians	Paul	around 55
Galatians	Paul	around 49
Ephesians	Paul	around 60
Philippians	Paul	around 61

Colossians	Paul	around 60
1 Thessalonians	Paul	50 - 51
2 Thessalonians	Paul	50 - 51
1 Timothy	Paul	around 62
2 Timothy	Paul	around 63
Titus	Paul	around 62
Philemon	Paul	around 60
Hebrews	Paul/Barnabas*	in 60s
James	James	40s or 50s
1 Peter	Peter	around 63
2 Peter	Peter	63 – 64
1 John	John	late 80s early 90s
2 John	John	late 80s early 90s
3 John	John	late 80s early 90s
Jude	Jude	between 60 to 80 AD
Revelation	John	late 80s early 90s

* There is some disagreement among the Biblical scholars as to the degree of certainty of these names and dates.

The Holy Bible is God's recorded word to mankind that reveals God's nature, God's will and God's plan for us!

SOME IMPORTANT QUESTIONS

Do we have those 'original autographs' penned by the inspired men of God with us now?

The answer is 'no.' (Even the original autographs of the Qur'an are also not available now! Since the materials of the original autographs coming from the inspired men of God had worn out due to repeated use as well as hundreds of years of exposure to the eroding effect of the air and light copies have been made of them several times over through the subsequent centuries. This is the case with almost all of ancient literature, secular or religious. The same is true even for the materials on which the Qur'an was originally written when the Islamic prophet Muhammad supposedly first recited the Qur'anic revelations to his followers. According to Islamic sources, the original Qur'an was written on parchments, leaf-stalks of date palms, scapula etc. [*Sahih al-Bukhari*, Volume 6, Book 60, Number 201; *Sahih Hadith, Al Bukhari*, Vol. 6, p.478], but none of them survived!)

Does God need the 'original autographs' in order to be able to protect His word?

Again, the answer is 'no!'

Is God able to keep His word intact regardless of how long the materials on which they were originally written exist?

The answer is a resounding 'yes!'

Does that mean the original word of God without changes and errors is still available?

That's precisely the case!

How certain can we be about that?

One of the objective ways to discover the answer to the above question is the academic approach. This approach employs critical textual analysis to arrive at the best possible scenario for the reliability of the texts that the Christian faith rests on. This is the standard method employed in testing all the ancient texts in general. Through this method by examining their ancient extant copies both the Bible and the Qur'an are declared by the scholars as trustworthy in representing their original messages.

However, it is common knowledge in the field of textual analysis that any ancient writing that survived, either in the form of a single copy or multiple copies, itself cannot offer any conclusive proof to be declared as perfectly representing the original to the precision of one hundred percent certainty. But for all practical purposes such precision is considered unwarranted in the field of textual analysis.

For a hyper skeptic, theoretically both the Bible and Qur'an may not have been preserved perfectly with mathematical precision and therefore neither can be declared with certainty as accurately representing its originals. In reality, there are only two ways by which we can know for certain if either of them is perfectly representing the original. First one is by comparing them with their originals. Second one is by ascertaining the genuine divine promise for the preservation.

We have originals of neither of these two books with us today, as already stated. Therefore, the first way is impractical to put to the test. Now we are left with only the second one. Both books have claims to the divine promise of preservation. The following are but a few divine promises of the preservation of the Bible:

"Your word, LORD, is eternal; it stands firm in the heavens." (O.T: Ps.119:89)
"Look in the scroll of the LORD and read: None of these will be missing, not one will lack her mate. For it is his mouth that has given the order, and his Spirit will gather them together." (O.T.: Is.34:16)
"The grass withers and the flowers fall, but the word of our God endures forever." (O.T.: Is.40:8)
"so is my word that goes out from my mouth: It will not return to me empty, but will accomplish what I desire and achieve the purpose for which I sent it." (O.T.: Is.55:11)
"For truly I tell you, until heaven and earth disappear, not the smallest letter, not the least stroke of a pen, will by any means disappear from the Law until everything is accomplished." (N.T.: Matt.5:18)
"Heaven and earth will pass away, but my words will never pass away." (N.T.: Lk.21:33)
And a few more…(cf. Is.59:21; Heb.2:2; 1Pet.1:25)

Even the author of the Quran also makes similar claims:

"Lo! We, even We, reveal the Reminder, and lo! We verily are its Guardian." (S.15:9)
"Nay, but it is a glorious Qur'an. On a guarded tablet." (S.85:21-22)

Since these two books are not compatible with each other on many counts, it stands to reason that only one of them can have the genuine divine promise of preservation. Logically, both books cannot be truly from God, either one of them is from God or none of them is from God. First, let's see if the claim of the Bible to its divine preservation is true.

Below, I offer three strands of evidence for the claim of the Bible that it has the divine promise of preservation, namely, evidence from ancient manuscripts, evidence from reason and evidence from divine inspiration.

(1) Evidence from ancient manuscripts

Old Testament (O.T.):

The Jewish Scriptures (*Tanakh*) are known as the Old Testament to Christians. Thirty-nine individual books of the Jewish Scriptures form the O.T. It is mainly divided into three parts as Jesus alluded to in the New Testament (Lk.24:44):

I. The Law (Law of Moses or Pentateuch or the first five books of the O.T.)
II. Prophets (Former and Latter)
III. Writings (Poetic, Scrolls, Prophetic and Historical)

The O.T. was written over a period of thousand years (1450 B.C. – 450 B.C.) by several men of God. Its faithful transmission is evident from the following major textual sources:

a. *Masoretic Text* (Prepared by Jewish scribes in the 6th century AD.) The oldest available MSS dated from the 10th Century reside in the Public Library of Leningrad, Russia.
b. *Septuagint* (Greek translation copies of the O.T. in the 3rd Century BC.) The oldest available MSS copies are dated from the 1st Century BC to the 1st Century AD. The oldest manuscript fragment from 2nd century BC is currently housed

at the John Rylands Library in Manchester, UK and the second oldest manuscript fragment from 1st or 2nd century BC is housed at the Societe Royale de Papyrologie, Cairo, Egypt.
  c. *Codex Vaticanus* (the Greek Bible—O.T. & N.T.). The oldest available manuscript copies dated at 4th century BC are housed at the Vatican Library in Rome.
  d. *Latin Vulgate* (Latin translation of the O.T. by Jerome in the 5th Century AD.) The oldest available MSS copies dated from the 6th Century AD are housed at the Laurentian Library in Florence, Italy.
  e. *Samaritan Pentateuch* (Produced in the 5th Century AD.) The oldest available MSS dated from the 12th Century AD are housed at Cambridge University Library, UK.
  f. *Syriac Version* (Syrian translation of the O.T. made in the 3rd Century AD.) The oldest available MSS are dated from the 5th and the 6th Century AD. The earliest dated manuscript copies from the 5th Century are housed at British Library, London.
  g. *Dead Sea Scrolls* (Produced and also available ranging from the 3rd Century BC to the 1st Century AD). Some of the MSS dated from 2nd to 1st century BC are at Hebrew University in Jerusalem, Israel.

Despite the presence of variant readings authenticity, reliability and faithful transmission of the O.T. is confirmed from the above major surviving ancient manuscripts (MSS). Apart from these ancient manuscripts there are a huge number of references to the O.T. in ancient historical writings as well as the writings of the Christian leaders along with a significant amount of quotations in the New Testament itself reiterate the trustworthiness of the O.T.

New Testament (N.T.):
  The Christian Scriptures that are commonly known as the New Testament are given in twenty-seven individual books. These are written in Greek by several men of God over a period of 40- 50 years (50 A.D. – 95 A.D.). Its preservation is evident from the abundance of its available ancient manuscripts today.
  Christian scholars Norman L. Geisler and Abdul Saleeb summarize the gist of the academic approach in these words, "Furthermore, Muslim rejection of the New Testament is contra-

ry to the overwhelming manuscript evidence. All the Gospels are preserved in the Chester Beatty Papyri, dated about A.D. 250. And almost the entire New Testament exists in the Vaticanus Ms. (B) that dates from about A.D. 325-50. In addition there are over, 5,300 other manuscripts of the New Testament dating from the second century A.D. to the fifteenth century A.D., hundreds of which are from before the time of Muhammad, that confirm the same substantial text of the whole New Testament in Muhammad's day." (Norman L. Geisler and Abdul Saleeb, *Answering Islam*, Baker Books, 1993, p.213.)

According to the eminent Christian apologist Dr. James White we have 12 manuscripts within the first 100 years after the writing of the NT; all are fragmentary but grand total they represent a majority of the books of NT and about $4/10^{th}$ of the text. Apart from this we have 120 hand-written manuscript copies of the NT within the first 300 years (50 A.D. – 350 A.D.) after the writing of the NT, some of which are full books of the whole NT.

The late Sir Frederic Kenyon the director of the British Museum wrote, "The text of the Bible is certain; especially is this the case with the New Testament. The number of manuscripts of the New Testament, of early translations from it, and of quotations from it in the oldest writers of the church, is so large that it is practically certain that the true reading of every doubtful passage is preserved in some one or other of these ancient authorities. This can be said of no other ancient book." (Sir Frederick Kenyon, *Our Bible and the Ancient Manuscripts*, [New York: Harper and Row, 1941], p. 23.)

Questions to Muslims

Question#1: Dear Muslims, if you are not convinced with the abundant ancient manuscript evidence for the accuracy of the Biblical transmission what else would convince you of that fact?
Question#2: If some Christian ruler similar to Uthaman had collected all the copies of the Holy Bible and made a standardized version and then destroyed the rest would that be sufficient to prove that the Holy Bible is preserved till today?
Queston#3: How does the fact that the ancient manuscripts of the Holy Bible do contain variant readings itself prove conclusively that none of them

is exactly representing the original?

Question#4: If you think the ancient manuscripts of the Holy Bible are mere human accounts or writings, then how come Allah's words were not preserved till now while the writings of mere human beings are preserved for more than two thousand years?

(2) Evidence from reason

The second evidence is demonstrated below through a series of logically connected axioms. This approach can be termed as the 'religious approach' or 'theistic approach.' In this approach it becomes apparent through the logical conclusions that the texts of the Christian faith are as solid as the ground we stand on.

- God as the all-powerful and sovereign Lord exists.
- God has the ability to communicate or speak in a language mankind can understand.
- He spoke through His chosen people by means of inspiration.
- All those words given by men of God under divine inspiration are God's word or message to mankind.
- The Jewish Scriptures (the Law, the Prophets, the Psalms etc.) and the Christian Scriptures (the Gospels, the Acts of Apostles, the Letters and the Book of Revelation) together form the word of God.
- These Scriptures are inerrant, complete and unalterable for they originated from God!
- Scriptures, as given in their original form, are intended for the generations during the times they were given as well as the generations in the future. This is why they are being preserved by the Almighty in accordance to His own promises (Psalm 19:7; 119:89; Isaiah 30:8, 40:8; Mat.5:18; Lk.21:33; Heb.2:2; 1Pet.1:25).

- Scriptures are preserved either at least in one of the copies extant or spread across the existing whole body of the ancient manuscript copies numbering in hundreds if not thousands coming from the first to sixth centuries of the Common Era.
- The collection of these Scriptures that came through the surviving copies into one volume is called the Holy Bible or God's word.
- The Holy Bible, even after translated into any language in the world, continues to retain and communicate the power and truth of God's message to mankind. That is why the translations of the Holy Bible in any language are regarded as God's word.
- The translations of the Holy Bible in other languages are not perfect in form and substance, but will have been affected by translation limitations and translators' understandings. This has given way to various translations in English alone that are called 'versions.' The variations in these translations have no bearing on the copies of the original language manuscripts or on the contents of the original autographs themselves.
- As far as the original form and substance of the Holy Bible are concerned the available ancient manuscript copies and the divine providence have confirmed them beyond any shadow of doubt.

The above logically connected line of thinking confirms the reliability of the transmission of the Bible through a couple millennia of human history.

Some Muslim apologists seek to raise objections to the above Christian understanding. The following three dialogues focus on the objections and expose the fallacious stand Muslim apologists take in this area:

The Holy Bible: Muslim Objections and Christian Responses

Dialogue#1

Muslim apologist: You don't have the original autographs of the Bible, do you? First show me the originals, if you want to say that the Bible is God's word.

Christian: Well, it is true that we don't have the original autographs of the Bible with us. Is that the only criterion that ensures whether we have God's words still with us?

Muslim apologist: Ok, I see your point. But, how else do you prove that you have God's words with you?

Christian: That's a good question. That's what we both need to figure out and agree upon. Because, not only you have the right to ask me that question, but I also have the right to ask you the same question about the Qur'an. Let's have the same standard and equal scales to measure both the Christian faith in the Bible as God's word and the Muslim faith in the Qur'an as Allah's word.

Questions to Muslims

Question#1: If you insist on showing the original autographs of the Holy Bible, then can you first show us the original autographs of the Qur'an that were written on palm leaves, white stones and shoulder bones during the time of Muhammad himself?

Question#2: If you don't have the original autographs of the Qur'an, why do you insist on seeing the original autographs of the Bible?

Dialogue#2

Muslim apologist: There are hundreds of thousands of variant readings in the copies of the Bible. That shows it is corrupted beyond recognition.

Christian: You mean just between any two different manuscripts or among the thousands of manuscripts of the Bible that we have today?

Muslim apologist: Oh yeah! It's not just between any two different manuscripts of the Bible.

Christian: The reality is there are thousands of ancient manuscripts of the Bible, some in parts and some as whole books. If we take into consideration all these available ancient manuscripts of the Bible, yes, there are hundreds of thousands of variant readings. But we should remember the fact that those who made these copies were scribes, but not divinely inspired writers.

Muslim apologist: But that's not the case with the Qur'an!

Christian: Well, you are comparing apples to oranges here. First, there are thousands of ancient manuscripts available today for the Bible even though it was given five hundred to two thousand years prior to the Noble Qur'an. Whereas, there are far fewer ancient manuscripts available today for the Qur'an in comparison to the Bible. Second, there are more than one hundred textual differences just between the ancient Samarkand manuscript and the modern Qur'an alone. If we compare the two modern versions of the Qur'an, Hafs version and Warsh version, we see more than thirteen hundred variations between these two alone! The fact is, no two ancient manuscript copies of the Qur'an are without a single variant. Please do not misunderstand my point here. This fact alone does not invalidate the Qur'an as God's words. But it does demonstrate to us that all ancient hand-written manuscripts are prone to variant readings no matter how meticulous the copyists may have been. Third, had we have similar number of ancient manuscripts for the Qur'an as the Bible, then the Qur'anic variant readings would have been far greater in number than in the case of the Bible! Finally, had someone in Christianity collected all the ancient copies and made just one standard version like the way Uthman the third Caliph in Islam did to the Qur'an, then the manuscripts of the Bible would have been without any variant readings unlike the Qur'an whose manuscripts have too many variant readings even after Uthman's purging of all the variant readings in its formative years.

Dialoguge#3

Muslim apologist: If God wanted to give his word to mankind he could have preserved it perfectly even through copyists.
Christian: Well, that's not the only way God has before Him to transmit His word through several generations. If it were the case, He would have done that through granting the inspiration even to the copyists. But He did not choose that way. By the way, the same is also said of the Qur'an, right?
Muslim apologist: Like what…?
Christian: If Allah wanted to give his Qur'an to mankind he would have preserved it by giving it exactly and perfectly same in every single ancient manuscript that we have now, but that is not the case!
Muslim apologist: Oh, I see!
Christian: The other important point we must bear in mind is God created all, loves all and gave His word to all. But that doesn't necessitate that His word should be exactly the same in each and every single copy that is ever made and must get as a whole into the hands of every single human being on this planet of earth.

(3) Evidence from divine inspiration

Divine inspiration ensures divine authentication and reliability. The Bible is divinely inspired. The following are some of the facts that attest to this truth:

Internal testimony: The Bible makes claims to its own divine inspiration (2Timonty 3:16-17; 2Peter 1:20-21).

External testimony: Recognition of the contemporary believing community is the most important external testimony that the Bible has for its divine inspiration. The faithful passing down of the Scriptures is done by each generation starting from the time they were given. It is the testimony of the contemporaries of the Scriptures that caused the subsequent generations to give the Scriptures the place they deserved. All the books of the Bible thus possess the attestations of their contemporaries.

External Evidence: Any ancient book that claims to be without corruption ought to have enough manuscript evidences in support of its claim. No other ancient book, religious or historical, can come anywhere near to the Bible. We have now more than 25,000 manuscript copies, in parts or in whole books, all of them are from before 600 A.D. They are in different places and in different languages. If any corruption or change was intended then it had to be carried out in all those copies with the consent of all the owners of those copies which is an impossible task. The sheer number of manuscripts that are available for the Bible not only prevent the corruption but also affirm its reliable transmission down the centuries.

Unity & coherence: The sixty-six individual books of the Bible were written by different men of God under divine inspiration in different ages (over a period of 1400 years) in different languages(Hebrew, Aramaic and Greek) and places (Asia, Africa and Europe), yet they all form a coherent unity complementing each other in describing various themes and subjects. This kind of miracle is possible only under divine power.

Fulfilled prophecy: A number of prophecies given both in the O.T. and the N.T. i.e. the Holy Bible, are fulfilled with remarkable accuracy.

The Bible is the only religious book in existence that dared to detail thousands of prophecies thousands of years before they actually came to pass. Many prophecies have already been fulfilled, some are being fulfilled even in our times, and some are yet to be fulfilled. As the Book of the Almighty God, only this Book enjoys the enormous amount of prophetic revelations (25% of the whole Bible) and also it has no rival in its fulfilled prophecy. These predictions, recorded sometimes hundreds of years in advance of their happening, are fulfilled in minute details. The God of the Bible is challenging other so-called gods, prophets and religions:

"Present your case...let them bring forth and declare to us what is going to take place...or announce to us what is coming. Declare the things that are going to come afterward that we may know... Indeed you are nothing, And your work is nothing; He who chooses you is an abomination (Is. 41: 21-24). Then He says: *"For I am God, and there is no other; I am God and there is none like Me, <u>declaring the end from the beginning</u>, and from ancient times things that are not yet done, saying, 'My council shall stand, and I will do all my pleasure"* (Isaiah 46:9-10). Following are a few of His predictions and their fulfilments:

 (a) Alexander the great–About Alexander the great and his four successors (350 B.C. -150 B.C.) was prophesied in the Bible (Daniel 8:1-18, 20-22--around 600 B.C) 200 years earlier to the actual happenings of the events.
 (b) Historical cities—Cities like Tyre, Sidon, Samaria, Petra and Edom have perished in the history just the way they were foreseen in the prophecies of the Bible centuries earlier.
 (c) The Messiah–More than 400 prophecies were written concerning the coming 'Messiah' in the Holy Book. These had been written several hundred years before the birth of Jesus Christ and were fulfilled in the birth, life, death and resurrection of Jesus Christ.
 (d) The Jewish temple—Both the first and the second temple of the Jews were destroyed as they were predicted in the prophecies of the Bible. The destruction of the first temple was prophesied around 950 B.C. (1Kings 9:8) and its fulfillment took place in 560 B.C. (2Kings 25:9). Then the destruction of the second temple was prophesied by Jesus

Christ (Matthew 24:2) in 30 A.D. and after 40 years i.e. in 70 A.D., it was completely destroyed, exactly the way Jesus described its fate.

Cross-authentication: Divine inspiration came through several anointed men of God who authenticated one another (Matt.5:17; Mk.9:12, 12:26; Lk.16:16; 2Cor.13:3,10; Eph.3:1-6; 1Thess.2:13; 2Thess.2:13-15; [1Tim.5:18 cf.Duet.25:4 & Lk.10:7]; 2Tim.3:16; 1Pet.1:10-12; 2Pet.1:21, 3:1-2, 15-16; Rev.1:1-3, 9-19).

Self-sufficiency: The Bible is self-sufficient in the areas of context, chronology, interpretation and prescription of its contents. It does not depend on human traditions - like the Qur'an on the Hadiths - in these areas.

Fundamental questions addressed: It answers all the queries related to origin, meaning, faith, experience, practice and destiny without any recourse to external sources or human traditions like the Hadiths in Islam.

Scientific accuracy: It is not a systematic scientific manual. However, wherever it alludes to science it makes appropriate observations (Eg. Job.26:7,10; Prov.8:27; Is. 40:22; Lk.17:34-36).

Although the Bible transcends science and nature in its accounts - affirming its supernatural origin - it is yet inclusive of the scientific dimension as well. Where the Bible speaks on matters of science, it does so using simple but appropriate terminology. Some of the examples of future scientific discoveries and inventions that are foreseen in the Bible more than 2500 years earlier are given below:

(a) **Discoveries**
   i. The position of the earth **in space**–Job 26:7 (2000 B.C.) "*He hangs the earth on nothing.*"
   ii. About the **core** of the earth–Job 28:5 (2000 B.C.) "*The earth, from it comes food, and underneath it is turned up as fire.*"
   iii. About the **mass** of the air–Job 28:25 (2000 B.C.) "God imparted *weight to the wind*"
   iv. The **roundness** of the earth–Isaiah 40:22 (750 B.C.) "*It is He* (God) *who enthroned above the circle of the earth.*"
   v. The **significance** of blood—Leviticus 17:11 (1500 B.C.),

"For the life of the flesh is in the blood."

The blood carries water and nourishment to every cell, maintains the body's temperature, and removes the waste material of the body's cells. The blood also carries oxygen from the lungs throughout the body. In 1616, William Harvey discovered that blood circulation is the key factor in physical life, confirming what the Bible revealed 3,000 years earlier.

vi. The **number of stars**—Jeremiah 33:22 (550 B.C.), *"As the host of heaven cannot be numbered, nor the sand of the sea measured, so will I multiply the descendants of David My servant and the Levites who minister to Me."*

According to scientists, even today we do not know exactly how many stars there are. Only about 3000 can be seen with the naked eye on a cloudless night sky. Scientists have estimated that there are about 10^{21} stars—which is a mindboggling number.

vii. Each star is **unique**—1 Corinthians 15:41 (55 A.D.) *"There is one glory of the sun, another glory of the moon, and another glory of the stars; for one star differs from another star in glory."* (1 Corinthians 15:41)

All stars look alike to the naked eye. But only an analysis of their light spectra reveals through the modern scientific methods that each is unique and different from all others.

viii. Creation made of **invisible elements**—Hebrews 11:3 (65 A.D.) *"Through faith we understand that the worlds were framed by the Word of God, so that things which are seen were not made of things which do appear."*

An experienced electronic engineer from Tamil Nadu, India sheds more light on this truth:

"The Higgs Boson is a sub-atomic particle, the idea of which was mooted in 1961 by Peter Higgs and Satyendra Nath Bose. This was then a theory but now has been confirmed as a reality. This sub-atomic particle having no mass has a property of arresting random movement (speed of light) of atoms to form matter of different shapes and sizes having different masses. On earth these masses of matter combined with gravity provide weight to objects. Thus, the Higgs Boson having no **mass (invisible)** is responsible for producing matter (visible). Let us compare this discovery with what is written in Scriptures 2000 years ago according to Hebrews 1:3 "By faith we understand that the Universe was formed at God's command so that what is seen was not made out of what was visible." *'What is seen'* is **matter** which has **mass** and the expression *'was not made out of what was visible'* simply means it was made out of what was invisible which we understand today is **The Higgs Boson."** (Dr.Rajkumar Ramachandran)

ix. Oceans and seas contain **springs**—Job 38:16 (2000 B.C.) "Have you journeyed to the <u>springs of the sea</u> or walked in the recesses of the deep?"

(b) **Inventions**

i. Modern **Travel** and **Knowledge**—Daniel 12:4 (500 B.C.) *"in the last days, <u>many will go back and forth, and knowledge will increase</u>"*.

ii. **Tunnels** and **Dams**—Job 28:10,11 (2000 B.C.) "Man <u>hews out channels through the rocks…dams up the stream from flowing</u> and what is hidden he brings out to the light".

Apart from the above few there are number of others hinted in the Bible concerning the anatomy, biology, oceanography, cosmology, automobiles, aerodynamics, etc. to which we in the modern world can relate.

Archeological conformity: The archaeological evidence in support of the Bible in general is overwhelming. In the past 150 years Biblical archeological findings have uncovered places, kingdoms, names, records of events, cities, names of false gods and goddesses, letters and Codices that have confirmed the accuracy of the accounts of the Holy Bible. An archaeologist summed it up like this, "The geography of the 'Holy Bible' lands and visible remains of antiquity were gradually recorded until today more than 25,000 sites within this region (Middle East) and dating to Old Testament times, in their broadest sense, have been located…" Besides the thousands of archaeological confirmations of the Bible, no archaeological find - in an eminent archaeologist's words - has ever been made that contradicts the history of the Bible.

Both O.T. and N.T. are given under divine inspiration. Its preservation has been assured by the Almighty Himself as given in Ps.119:89, Is.34:16, 40:8, 55:11, 59:21, Matt.5:18, 1Pet.1:25.

All the above three strands of evidence confirm conclusively that the Bible's claim to its divine preservation is genuine and trustworthy.

The Holy Bible: Muslim Objections and Christian Responses

UNIQUENESS OF THE HOLY BIBLE IN COMPARISON TO THE NOBLE QUR'AN

Area of distinction	The Holy Bible	The Noble Qur'an
The first ever book printed on Gutenberg printing press	Johann Gutenberg holds the distinction of being the inventor of the movable-type printing press. In 1455, Gutenberg produced what is considered to be the first book ever printed: a Latin language Bible, printed in Mainz, Germany.	It doesn't have this privilege!
The first ever book that was taken into space and read	On the Christmas Eve of 1968 from 200,000 miles away in space Jim Lovell, one of the three astronauts on Apollo 8 spacecraft, read from the first chapter of the first book of the Bible— *"In the beginning God created the heavens and the earth..."* (Genesis chapter 1)	It doesn't have this privilege!
The first ever book that was taken on to the moon	The "Lunar Bible," a little square sheet of microfilm, just an inch and a half on a side, carried to the surface of the moon by astronaut Edgar Mitchell on Apollo 14 in February 1971.	It doesn't have this privilege
Number of individual books/chapters	66 individual books (with overall context, chronology and meaningful transition and harmony it offers clarity to the reader)	114 individual chapters (without context, chronology and meaningful transition it fails to offer clarity to the reader)
Number of persons through whom the book was given	30 Jewish men of YHWH/God such as prophets, priests, rulers and singers, and 8 Christian men of YHWH/God such as Apostles and Evangelists. This fact alone eliminates all possibilities for self-serving pseudo-revelations coming from individuals. It also underscores the supernatural dimension of its origin through its awe-inspiring unity weaved together by such a diversity of writers over a period of 1500 years!	One prophet of the Qur'anic Allah (this fact undercuts the surety that so-called revelations are not self-serving pseudo-revelations)
Number of writers involved	38 inspired writers (prophets, priests, apostles, evangelists etc.) contributed to the written form of the Bible.	Around 40 Muslim scribes under Muhammad contributed to the written form of the Qur'an. All of them

			were non-inspired individuals.
Period of time taken for the whole revelation	1540 years (1445 B.C – 95 A.D.)		22 years (610-632 A.D.)
Manner of collection	The 66 books were collected from the inspired writers. But they were not collected under the controlling supervision of a single human or human authority. Yet, miraculously they all have intricate harmony among themselves confirming the divine inspiration and sovereignty in their production, collection and gathering up into one Holy Book.		114 chapters were collected from non-inspired scribes. Even these collections were made under the controlling supervision of one man Zaid and one human authority (first Abu Bakr's and second Uthman's), yet there are many inconsistencies and conflicts among themselves.
Available original materials on which the revelations first recorded	None are available today!		None are available today!
Oldest manuscripts available now	i) Old Testament fragments in Greek from 150-70 B.C. (Rylands Papyrus 458); ii) New Testament fragments from 100 A.D. (Chester Beatty Papyrus II)		From 670-715 A.D. (Sanaa Manuscripts)
Significant old manuscript copies or fragments available today	i) Septuagint (200 – 100 B.C.) ii) Dead Sea Scrolls (150-100 B.C.) iii) Codex Vaticanus (325-350 A.D.) iv) Codex Sinaiticus (375-400 A.D.) v) Codex Washingtonianus (450 A.D.) vi) Codex Alexandrinus (450 A.D.)		i) Sana Manuscripts (670-715 A.D.) ii) Codex Parisino-Petropolitanus (690-720 A.D.) iii) Topkapi Manuscript (710-750 A.D.) iv) Cairo Mushaf (720-25 A.D.) v) Samarkand Manuscript (780-810 A.D.) vi) Ma'il Script Manuscript (790 A.D.)

The Holy Bible: Muslim Objections and Christian Responses

Languages used for writing the book	Three: Hebrew, Aramaic and Greek	One: Arabic
Places where the book was given/written	Three continents: *Asia*, *Africa* and *Europe*!	Two cities: *Mecca* and *Medina* in Saudi Arabia.
Translations into other languages	Translations of the Bible available as of 2013: Full Bible in 513 languages; only N.T. in 1294 languages; some scripture portions in 1010 languages!	As of 2014 the Qur'an has been translated into 107 languages.
Sufficiency	The final teachings of the Bible i.e. New Testament, that came in the last stage of its progressive revelation, are sufficient for faith, experience, practice and hope till the end of time.	The Qur'an alone is not sufficient for Muslims' faith, experience, practice and hope. Much of this comes from traditions called 'Hadiths.'
Original language limitations	The message of the Bible possesses both divine truth and divine power which are by no means restricted only to its original languages. Through its influence, even in its translated form in more than 1300 languages of the world, it has been transforming millions of lives for good every year. A significant percentage of the Muslims who have become the followers of Christ took that decision just by reading the contents of the Bible in their respective native languages.	The so-called beauty and uniqueness of the Qur'an are limited only to the Arabic language in which it was given.
Geo-political limitations	The Bible is feared and has been banned in many Islamic nations even as of today. Many Christians have suffered persecution for carrying Bibles in Islamic nations. In spite of this the Bible is penetrating into those restricted places and bringing many people to Christ.	Qur'an doesn't have such limitations and effects.

2. MUSLIMS' UNDERSTANDING OF THE WORD OF GOD

As far as the Islamic faith is concerned the *Tawraat, Zaboor, Injeel* and Qur'an are God's word or Allah's word (Arabic: Allah=The God) to mankind. All these books are sent to mankind from Allah through prophets and messengers.

In classical Islam the Jewish Scriptures (Tanakh/Old Testament) are referred to as the *Tawraat* and *Zaboor* or the Previous Scriptures, while the Christian Scriptures (New Testament) are referred to as the *Injeel* or the Previous Scriptures. As far as the Arab Christians are concerned even from before the birth of Islam the Holy Bible is the compilation of the *Tawraat* (Torah), *Zaboor* (Pslams) and *Injeel* (Gospel/N.T.).

According to the Qur'an the Jewish Scriptures (Tawraat and Zaboor) and the Christian Scriptures (Injeel/N.T.) were actually sent down from Allah (S. 5:43-47).

Qur'an: Al Maidah (The Table Spread) 5:44 & 46

"لِلَّذِينَ هَادُوا فِيهَا هُدًى وَنُورٌ يَحْكُمُ بِهَا النَّبِيُّونَ الَّذِينَ أَسْلَمُوا إِنَّا أَنزَلْنَا التَّوْرَاةَ"
"تَخْشَوُا اسْتُحْفِظُوا مِن كِتَابِ اللَّهِ وَكَانُوا عَلَيْهِ شُهَدَاءَ فَلاَ وَالرَّبَّانِيُّونَ وَالأَحْبَارُ بِمَا قَلِيلاً وَمَن لَّمْ يَحْكُم بِمَا أَنزَلَ اللَّهُ فَأُولَٰئِكَ هُمُ النَّاسَ وَاخْشَوْنِ وَلاَ تَشْتَرُوا بِآيَاتِي ثَمَنًا الْكَافِرُونَ"

"Lo! <u>We did reveal **the Torah**</u>, wherein is guidance and a light, by which the prophets who surrendered (unto Allah) judged the Jews, and the rabbis and the priests (judged) by such of Allah's Scripture as they were bidden to observe, and thereunto were they witnesses. So fear not mankind, but fear Me. And My revelations for a little gain. Whoso judgeth not by that which Allah hath revealed: such are disbelievers."

The Holy Bible: Muslim Objections and Christian Responses

"التَّوْرَاةِ وَآتَيْنَاهُ الإِنجِيلَ بِعِيسَى ابْنِ مَرْيَمَ مُصَدِّقًا لِمَا بَيْنَ يَدَيْهِ مِنَ وَقَفَّيْنَا عَلَىٰ آثَارِهِم"
"لِلْمُتَّقِينَ لِمَا بَيْنَ يَدَيْهِ مِنَ التَّوْرَاةِ وَهُدًى وَمَوْعِظَةً فِيهِ هُدًى وَنُورٌ وَمُصَدِّقًا"

"*And We caused Jesus, son of Mary, to follow in their footsteps, <u>confirming</u> that which was (revealed) before him in **the Torah**, and <u>We bestowed on him **the Injeel**</u> (Gospel) wherein is guidance and a light, confirming that which was (revealed) before it in the Torah - a guidance and an admonition unto those who ward off (evil).*"

Qur'an: Al-Isra (The Night Journey) 17:55

عَلَىٰ بَعْضٍ   السَّمَاوَاتِ وَالأَرْضِ   وَلَقَدْ فَضَّلْنَا بَعْضَ النَّبِيِّينَ وَرَبُّكَ أَعْلَمُ بِمَن فِي
"وَآتَيْنَا دَاوُودَ زَبُورًا"

"*And thy Lord is Best Aware of all who are in the heavens and the earth. And we preferred some of the prophets above others, and <u>unto David We gave</u> **the Zaboor** (Psalms).*"

However, in reality today's Muslims circumvent this Qur'anic declaration in its substance and reduce it to a mere lip-service. As a result, there arose at least three differing views within the Muslim community with regard to the Judeo-Christian Scriptures i.e. the Holy Bible. One view holds that the Tawraat, Zaboor and Injeel were originally sent down from Allah as Allah's word, but later they all got corrupted or tampered with and are therefore unreliable. In other words, today's Bible is the collection of the corrupted and unreliable books that were originally sent down from Allah. This is the popular view among Muslims.

The second view holds that the Tawraat, Zaboor and Injeel were from Allah, but all those original books of Allah are no longer in existence now. What Jews and Christians possess now as the Holy Bible is the collection of different books that were produced by mere human authors, but not the original books of Allah.

The third view holds that the Holy Bible is from Allah for it comprises of the previous Scriptures the Tawraat, Zaboor and Injeel, that were sent down from Allah. However, now that Allah gave the final book Qur'an the Holy Bible is no longer relevant and has become obsolete. According to this view the Qur'an supersedes and abrogates the Holy Bible as the final revelation from Allah.

Muslims believe that the Qur'an they read in this world is only a replica of the Qur'an that exists in heaven alongside of Allah without a beginning and end as the eternal speech of Allah. The heavenly Qur'an exists alongside of Allah but not same as Allah. A Sunni Muslim scholar sums up this belief when he said, "Ahl al-Sunna agree one and all that the Qur'an is the pre-existent, pre-eternal, uncreated Speech of Allah Most High on the evidence of the Qur'an, the Sunna, and faith-guided reason." (Dr.G.F.Haddad, *The Glorious Quran,* p.1)

Qur'an consists of 114 chapters called *surahs*. The surahs of the Qur'an are arranged not chronologically, but in descending order from the longest to the shortest. Exempted from this rule is the first surah. Each surah has a name. For example, the first surah is called Surah *Al-Fatiha* (The Opening). Likewise, the surah 19 is named after Mary (Mariyam) the mother of Isa the Islamic Jesus. The longest surah of the Qur'an is the Surah *Al-Baqara* (The Cow) with 286 verses and the shortest one is the Surah *Al-Kawthar* (abundance) with just 3 verses. Muslims believe that the Qur'an they read is exactly the same Qur'an that Muhammad gave them fourteen centuries ago. Yet, ironically the total number of the words in the Arabic Qur'an according to one estimate is 77,430, another estimate is 77,277, still another estimate is 77,437, one more estimate is 77,439, and still one more estimate is 77,934!

The Qur'an as a book is a little shorter than the New Testament in length. The 96th surah was supposedly revealed first when the Islamic prophet Muhammad started to receive the 'revelations.' The first surah *Al-Fatiha* is considered by some Muslims as equal to the third of the Qur'an while others as the rest of the Qur'an. The contents of the Qur'an were given by the Islamic prophet Muhammad to his followers neither all at once nor as meaningful chunks of information, but in piecemeal on different occasions. These piecemeal revelations were given in two different places—Mecca and Medina. Hence some of them called Meccan Surahs and the others Medinan Surahs.

Muslims believe that the Qur'an was revealed through the angel Gabriel to Muhammad in the Arabic language over a period of 22 years i.e. 610-632 A.D. They also believe even in heaven it is preserved in Arabic language. Hence, they hold the view that their holy book Qur'an cannot be translated into other languages. This is why Muslims consider the translations of the Qur'an in other languages only as a 'meaning of the Qur'an!' It goes without saying that it is an undisputed fact that the translated versions of the Qur'an in other languages do not have the same beauty or uniqueness of the Arabic version of the Qur'an. The same can be said of any other book particularly of poetic nature!

About 71 verses of the Qur'an refer to Isa the Islamic Jesus. He is mentioned by name more than 25 times in the entire Qur'an. He is also given the title *Masih* (Messiah) 11 times in the Qur'an. However, the Qur'an fails to explain what the title *Masih* means! Interestingly, the name of Muhammad is mentioned only four times (S. 3:144; 33:40; 47:2; 48:29) and *Ahmad* just once in the Qur'an (S. 61:6). *Ahmad* in Arabic means 'the praised one.' This is believed to be another name of Muhammad.

The Islamic Jesus' mother Mary (Maryam) is the only woman mentioned in the entire Qur'an by name; a whole surah is named after her. In contrast, neither Muhammad's mother Amina, who died six years after Muhammad's birth, nor his father Abdullah, who had died several weeks before Muhammad's birth, is mentioned in it. The Qur'an acknowledges divine intervention in Jesus' birth, death and resurrection. It even attributes miracles such as healing the sick, raising the dead back to life etc. (S. 3:42-55) to Jesus. In fact, the Qur'an attributes theologically highly significant titles such as *Kalimatullah* (Word of Allah) and *Ruhullah* (Spirit of Allah) to Jesus (S. 3:45, 4:171). None of these privileges and honors was given to the Islamic prophet Muhammad himself. One should wonder why Jesus is exalted so much even in the Qur'an. Of course, only the Injeel (the New Testament) can explain that satisfactorily and accurately.

In addition to Qur'an Muslims also need *Hadiths* (traditions composed and circulated among Muslims regarding Muhammad's life, sayings and actions that were codified a hundred and fifty years after Muhammad's death) for their belief, practice, experience and hope (more on the Hadiths in chapter 4). Qur'an and the *Sunnah* i.e. example of the prophet, together form two legs on which Islam stands. The Sunnah of Muhammad is found in the Islamic Hadith literature. According to a Muslim scholar, 'Hadith is integral to the Qur'an, since they are inseparably linked to each other. It is impossible to understand the Qur'an without reference to Hadith. The Qur'an is the message, and the Hadith is the explanation of the message by the Messenger himself.' (Sheikh Ahmad Kutty, *What is the significance of Hadith in Islam?*).

THE LIST OF THE SURAHS OF THE QUR'AN

No. of Surah	Chrono-logical order	Meaning of Surah name	Translitera-tion of Surah name	No. of verses	Location of revelation	Surah name in Arabic
1.	5	The Opening	Al-Fatiha	7	Mecca	سورة الفاتحة
2.	87	The Calf, The Cow	Al-Baqara	286	Medina	سورة البقرة
3.	89	The Family of Imran, The House of Imran	Al Imran	200	Medina	سورة آل عمران
4.	92	The Women	An-Nisa	176	Medina	سورة النساء
5.	112	The Food, The Repast	Al-Ma'ida	120	Medina	سورة المائدة
6.	55	The Cattle	Al-An'am	165	Mecca	سورة الأنعام
7.	39	The Heights, The Faculty of Discern-ment	Al-A'raf	206	Mecca	سورة الأعراف
8.	89	The Spoils of War	Al-Anfal	75	Medina	سورة الأنفال
9.	113	The Repen-tance	At-Tawba	129	Medina	سورة التوبة
10.	51	Jonah	Yunus	109	Mecca	سورة يونس
11.	52	Hud	Houd	123	Mecca	سورة هود
12.	53	Joseph	Yusuf	111	Mecca	سورة يوسف
13.	96	The Thunder	Ar-R'ad	43	Medina	سورة الرَّعد
14.	72	Abraham	Ibraheem	52	Mecca	سورة إبراهيم
15.	54	The Rocky Tract, The Stoneland, The Rock City	Al-Hijr	99	Mecca	سورة الحجر
16.	70	The Honey Bees, The Bee	An-Nahl	128	Mecca	سورة النحل

17.	50	The Night Journey	Al-Isra	111	Mecca	سورة الإسراء
18.	69	The Cave	Al-Kahf	110	Mecca	سورة الكهف
19.	44	Mary	Maryam	98	Mecca	سورة مريم
20.	45	Ta-Ha	Ta-Ha	135	Mecca	سورة طه
21.	73	The Prophets	Al-Anbiya	112	Mecca	سورة الأنبياء
22.	103	The Pilgrimage	Al-Hajj	78	Medina	سورة الحج
23.	74	The Believers	Al-Mu'minoon	118	Mecca	سورة المؤمنون
24.	102	The Light	An-Nour	64	Medina	سورة النّور
25.	42	The Criterion, The Standard of True and False	Al-Furqan	77	Mecca	سورة الفرقان
26.	47	The Poets	Ash-Shu'ara	127	Mecca	سورة الشعراء
27.	48	The Ant, The Ants	An-Naml	93	Mecca	سورة النمل
28.	49	The Narrations, The Stories	Al-Qasas	88	Mecca	سورة القصص
29	85	The Spider	Al-Ankabut	69	Mecca	سورة العنكبوت
30.	84	The Romans, The Byzantines	Ar-Roum	60	Mecca	سورة الروم
31.	57	Luqman	Luqman	34	Mecca	سورة لقمان
32.	75	The Prostration, Worship	As-Sajda	30	Mecca	سورة السجدة
33.	90	The Clans, The Confederates	Al-Ahzab	73	Medina	سورة الأحزاب
34.	58	Sheba	Saba	54	Mecca	سورة سبأ
35.	43	The Originator of Creation	Fatir	45	Mecca	سورة فاطر
36.	41	Yaseen	Yaseen	83	Mecca	سورة يس

37.	56	Those Who Set The Ranks	As-Saffat	182	Mecca	سورة الصَّافات
38.	38	Sad, one of the Arabic alphabets	Sad	88	Mecca	سورة ص
39.	59	The Crowds, The Troops	Az-Zumar	75	Mecca	سورة الزمر
40.	60	The Forgiver	Ghafir	85	Mecca	سورة غافر
41.	61	Expounded, Clearly Spelled out	Fussilat	54	Mecca	سورة فصّلت
42.	62	The Consultation, Counsel	Ash-Shura	53	Mecca	سورة الشورى
43.	63	The Ornament of Gold	Az-Zukhruf	89	Mecca	سورة الزخرف
44.	64	The Smoke	Ad-Dukhan	59	Mecca	سورة الدخان
45.	65	The Kneeling down, crouching	Al-Jathiya	37	Mecca	سورة الجاثية
46.	66	Winding Sand-tracts, The Sand Dunes	Al-Ahqaf	35	Mecca	سورة الأحقاف
47.	95	Muhammad	Muhammad	38	Medina	سورة محمَّد
48.	111	The Victory, Conquest	Al-Fath	29	Medina	سورة الفتح
49.	106	The Private Apartments, The Inner Apartments	Al-Hujurat	18	Medina	سورة الحُجُرات

50.	34	Qaf, one of the Arabic alphabet	Qaf	45	Mecca	سورة ق
51.	67	The Winnowing Winds, The Dust-Scattering Winds	Adh-Dhariyat	60	Mecca	سورة الذاريات
52.	76	The Mount, Mount Sinai	At-Tour	49	Mecca	سورة الطور
53.	23	The Star, The Unfolding	An-Najm	62	Mecca	سورة النجم
54.	37	The Moon	Al-Qamar	55	Mecca	سورة القمر
55.	97	The Most Merciful, The Most Gracious	Ar-Rahman	78	Medina	سورة الرحمن
56.	46	The Event, The Inevitable	Al-Waqi'a	96	Mecca	سورة الواقية
57.	94	The Iron	Al-Hadeed	29	Medina	سورة الحديد
58.	105	The Pleading Women	Al-Mujadila	22	Medina	سورة المجادلة
59.	101	The Mustering, Banishment	Al-Hashr	24	Medina	سورة الحشر
60.	91	The Examined One	Al-Mumtahana	13	Medina	سورة الممتحنة
61.	109	The Ranks, Battle Array	As-Saff	14	Medina	سورة الصّف
62.	110	The Congregation, Friday	Al-Jumu'aa	11	Medina	سورة الجمعة
63.	104	The Hypocrites	Al-Munafiqoun	11	Medina	سورة المنافقون

The Holy Bible: Muslim Objections and Christian Responses

64.	108	The Cheating, The Mutual Disillusion	At-Taghabun	18	Medina	سورة الـتغابن
65.	99	Divorce	At-Talaq	12	Medina	سورة الـطلاق
66.	107	The Prohibition	At-Tahreem	12	Medina	سورة الـتحريم
67.	77	The Dominion, Sovereignty	Al-Mulk	30	Mecca	سورة الـملك
68.	2	The Pen	Al-Qalam	52	Mecca	سورة الـقلم
69.	78	The Sure Reality	Al-Haqqa	52	Mecca	سورة الـحاقة
70.	79	The Ascending Stairways	Al-Ma'aarij	44	Mecca	سورة الـمعارج
71.	71	Noah	Nouh	28	Mecca	سورة نوح
72.	40	The Spirits, The Unseen Beings	Al-Jinn	28	Mecca	سورة الجن
73.	3	The Enfolded One	Al-Muzzammil	20	Mecca	سورة الـمـزّمَـل
74.	4	The One Wrapped Up, The Man Wearing a Cloak	Al-Muddathir	56	Mecca	سورة الـمَـدّثـر
75.	31	The Day of Resurrection	Al-Qiyama	40	Mecca	سورة الـقيامـة
76.	98	The Human, Man, Time	Al-Insan	31	Medina	سورة الإنسان
77.	33	Those Sent Forth, The Emissaries	Al-Mursalat	50	Mecca	سورة الـمرسلات

MUSLIMS' UNDERSTANDING OF THE WORD OF GOD | 53

78.	80	The Great News, The Tiding, The Announcement	An-Naba'	40	Mecca	سورة النبا
79.	81	Those Who Tear Out, Soul-Snatchers	An-Nazi'at	46	Mecca	سورة النازعات
80.	24	He Frowned	Abasa	42	Mecca	سورة عبس
81.	7	The Folding Up, The Overthrowing	At-Takweer	29	Mecca	سورة التكوير
82.	82	The Cleaving Asunder	Al-Infitar	19	Mecca	سورة الانفطار
83.	86	The Dealers in Fraud, The Cheats	Al-Mutaffifeen	36	Mecca	سورة المطففين
84.	83	The Rending Asunder, Splitting Open	Al-Inshiqaq	25	Mecca	سورة الانشقاق
85.	27	The Mansion of the Stars, Constellation	Al-Burooj	22	Mecca	سورة البروج
86.	36	The Morning Star	At-Tariq	17	Mecca	سورة الطارق
87.	8	The Most High	Al-A'la	19	Mecca	سورة الأعلى
88.	68	The Overwhelming Event	Al-Ghashiya	26	Mecca	سورة الغاشية

The Holy Bible: Muslim Objections and Christian Responses

89.	10	The Dawn, The Daybreak	Al-Fajr	30	Mecca	سورة الفجر
90.	35	The City, The Land	Al-Balad	20	Mecca	سورة البلد
91.	26	The Sun	Ash-Shams	15	Mecca	سورة الشمس
92.	9	The Night	Al-Lail	21	Mecca	سورة الليل
93.	11	The Forenoon, The Bright Morning Hours	Ad-Dhuha	11	Mecca	سورة الضحى
94.	12	The Opening-up of the Heart, Relief	Al-Inshirah	8	Mecca	سورة الشرح
95.	28	The Fig, The Fig Tree	At-Teen	8	Mecca	سورة التين
96.	1	Clot of Blood	Al-Alaq	19	Mecca	سورة العلق
97.	25	The Night of Degree, Fate	Al-Qadr	5	Mecca	سورة القدر
98.	100	The Clear Evidence	Al-Bayyina	8	Medina	سورة البينة
99.	93	The Earth-quake	Az-Zalzala	8	Medina	سورة الزلزلة
100.	14	The Charger, The War Horse	Al-adiyat	11	Mecca	سورة العاديات
101.	30	The Striking Hour	Al-Qaria	11	Mecca	سورة القارعة
102.	16	The Pilling Up, Compe-tition	At-Takathur	8	Mecca	سورة التكاثر
103.	13	The Declining Day, The Flight of Time	Al-Asr	3	Mecca	سورة العصر

104.	32	The Gossiper, The Slanderer	Al-Humaza	9	Mecca	سورة الـهمزة
105.	19	The Elephant	Al-Feel	5	Mecca	سورة الـفيل
106.	29	Quraysh	Quraysh	4	Mecca	سورة قريش
107.	17	Almsgiving, Small Kindness	Al-Maa'oun	7	Mecca	سورة الماعون
108.	15	Plenty, Abundance, The River in Paradise	Al-Kawthar	3	Mecca	سورة الـكوثر
109.	18	The Disbelievers, Those who Deny the Truth	Al-Kafiroun	6	Mecca	سورة الـكافرون
110.	114	The Help, Divine Support, Victory	An-Nasr	3	Medina	سورة الـنصر
111.	6	The Palm Fiber, The Twisted Strands	Al-Masad	5	Mecca	سورة الـمسد
112.	22	Purity of Faith	Al-Ikhlas	4	Mecca	سورة الإخلاص
113.	20	The Daybreak, Dawn	Al-Falaq	5	Mecca	سورة الـفلق
114.	21	Mankind, Men	Al-Nas	6	Mecca	سورة الـناس

The Holy Bible: Muslim Objections and Christian Responses

3. PROPBLEMS WITH MUSLIMS' POSITION

Muslim scholars from the second century of Islam i.e. the 8th century A.D., differed among themselves regarding their position about the Holy Bible. In this chapter we will see how the Qur'an judges various positions Muslims hold.

QUR'AN CONDEMNS MUSLIM POSITION

The three views of Muslims with regard to the Judeo-Christian Scriptures, the Holy Bible, are riddled with logical as well as historical problems. First and foremost, even their Qur'an rules out any possibility for the three views Muslims hold now. In fact, the Qur'an repeatedly claims that it came to confirm, not to correct or cancel or replace, the previous Scriptures i.e. Tawraat, Zaboor and Injeel.

Qur'an: Sura al-Imran (Family of Imran) 3:3
"نَزَّلَ عَلَيْكَ الْكِتَابَ بِالْحَقِّ مُصَدِّقًا لِمَا بَيْنَ يَدَيْهِ وَأَنزَلَ التَّوْرَاةَ وَالإِنجِيلَ"
"*He hath revealed unto thee (Muhammad) the Scripture with truth,* **confirming** *that which was (revealed) before it, even as He revealed* <u>the</u> **Torah** *and the* **Injeel** *(Gospel).*"

Qur'an: Sura al-Baqarah (The Cow) 2:91
وَيَكْفُرُونَ بِمَا وَرَاءَهُ وَهُوَ الْحَقُّ مُصَدِّقًا لِمَا مَعَهُمْ ۗ قُلْ فَلِمَ تَقْتُلُونَ أَنْبِيَاءَ اللَّهِ مِنْ قَبْلُ إِنْ كُنْتُمْ مُؤْمِنِينَ" "وَإِذَا قِيلَ لَهُمْ آمِنُوا بِمَا أَنْزَلَ اللَّهُ قَالُوا نُؤْمِنُ بِمَا أُنْزِلَ عَلَيْنَا
"*And when it is said unto them: Believe in that which Allah hath revealed, they say: We believe in that which was revealed unto us. And they disbelieve in that which cometh after it, though it is the truth* **confirming** *that which*

they possess. Say (unto them, O Muhammad): Why then slew ye the prophets of Allah aforetime, if ye are (indeed) believers?"

Second, the Qur'an puts Muslims under Allah's judgment, a painful punishment, if they make any distinction between the Qur'an and the previous Scriptures i.e. Tawrat, Zaboor and Injeel. Ironically, most of the Muslims often commit this sin without even realizing!

Qur'an: An-Nisa (The Women) 4:136

يَا أَيُّهَا الَّذِينَ آمَنُوا آمِنُوا بِاللهِ وَرَسُولِهِ وَالْكِتَابِ الَّذِي نَزَّلَ عَلَىٰ رَسُولِهِ وَالْكِتَابِ الَّذِي أَنزَلَ مِن قَبْلُ وَمَن يَكْفُرْ بِاللهِ وَمَلَائِكَتِهِ وَكُتُبِهِ وَرُسُلِهِ وَالْيَوْمِ الْآخِرِ فَقَدْ ضَلَّ ضَلَالًا بَعِيدًا"

"O ye who believe! Believe in Allah and His messenger and the Scripture which He hath revealed unto His messenger, and the Scripture which He revealed aforetime. Whoso disbelieveth in Allah and His angels and His scriptures and His messengers and the Last Day, he verily hath wandered far astray."

Qur'an: Ali Imran (Family of Imran) 3:84

قُلْ آمَنَّا بِاللهِ وَمَا أُنزِلَ عَلَيْنَا وَمَا أُنزِلَ عَلَىٰ إِبْرَاهِيمَ وَإِسْمَاعِيلَ وَإِسْحَاقَ وَيَعْقُوبَ وَالْأَسْبَاطِ وَمَا أُوتِيَ مُوسَىٰ وَعِيسَىٰ وَالنَّبِيُّونَ مِن رَّبِّهِمْ لَا نُفَرِّقُ بَيْنَ أَحَدٍ مِّنْهُمْ وَنَحْنُ لَهُ مُسْلِمُونَ"

"Say (O Muhammad): We believe in Allah and that <u>which is revealed unto us</u> and that which was revealed unto Abraham and Ishmael and Isaac and Jacob and the tribes, <u>and that which was vouchsafed unto Moses and Jesus and the prophets</u> from their Lord. <u>We make **no distinction between any of them**</u>, and unto Him we have surrendered."

Qur'an: Ghafir (The Forgiver) 40:70-72

الَّذِينَ كَذَّبُوا بِالْكِتَابِ وَبِمَا أَرْسَلْنَا بِهِ رُسُلَنَا فَسَوْفَ يَعْلَمُونَ إِذِ الْأَغْلَالُ فِي أَعْنَاقِهِمْ وَالسَّلَاسِلُ يُسْحَبُونَ فِي الْحَمِيمِ ثُمَّ فِي النَّارِ يُسْجَرُونَ"

"Those who **deny the Scripture** and that **wherewith We send Our messengers**. But they will come to know, When carcans are about their necks and chains. They are dragged Through boiling waters; then they are thrust into the Fire."

Third, the Qur'an affirms that the words of Allah cannot be

changed.

Qur'an: Al-An'am (The Cattle) 6:34 & 115

"نَصْرُنَا وَلَا قِبَلِكَ فصَبَرُوا عَلَىٰ مَا كُذِّبُوا وَأُوذُوا حَتَّىٰ أَتَاهُمْ وَلَقَدْ كُذِّبَتْ رُسُلٌ مِّن"
"نَّبَإِ الْمُرْسَلِينَ مُبَدِّلَ لِكَلِمَاتِ اللَّهِ وَلَقَدْ جَاءَكَ مِن"

"Rejected were the apostles before thee: with patience and constancy they bore their rejection and their wrongs, until Our aid did reach them: <u>there is none that can alter the words (and decrees) of God</u>. Already hast thou received some account of those apostles."

"وَتَمَّتْ كَلِمَتُ رَبِّكَ صِدْقًا وَعَدْلًا لَا مُبَدِّلَ لِكَلِمَاتِهِ وَهُوَ السَّمِيعُ الْعَلِيمُ"

"<u>Perfected is the Word of thy Lord</u> in truth and justice. <u>There is naught that can change His words</u>. He is the Hearer, the Knower."

Fourth, Qur'an commands Muslims - who are also the 'People of the Scriptures' along with Jews and Christians - to observe the Torah (Tawraat) and the Injeel (Gospel) as we can see below. But in reality how many Muslims actually believe, read and observe the Torah (Tawraat) and the Injeel (Gospel)? Almost none!

Qur'an: Al-Maidah (The Table Spread) 5:68

"وَمَا أُنزِلَ إِلَيْكُم مِّن لَسْتُمْ عَلَىٰ شَيْءٍ حَتَّىٰ تُقِيمُوا التَّوْرَاةَ وَالْإِنجِيلَ قُلْ يَا أَهْلَ الْكِتَابِ"
"تَأْسَ عَلَى الْقَوْمِ مِنْهُم مَّا أُنزِلَ إِلَيْكَ مِن رَّبِّكَ طُغْيَانًا وَكُفْرًا فَلَا رَبِّكَ وَلَيَزِيدَنَّ كَثِيرًا"
"الْكَافِرِينَ"

"*Say O <u>People of the Scripture</u>! Ye have naught (of guidance) till ye <u>observe the Torah and the Gospel</u> **and** <u>that which was revealed unto you from your Lord</u>. That which is revealed unto thee (Muhammad) from thy Lord is certain to increase the contumacy and disbelief of many of them. But grieve not for the disbelieving folk.*"

Regardless of the three divergent views held by different Muslims it is noteworthy to see that most of the Muslims from all schools of thought would go to great lengths to prove the authenticity of their religion, prophet and book based on the Biblical data by way of interpreting it as they see it fit to do their job. This kind of dishonest and illogical efforts made by some Muslims only prove that they are desperate to find some ways to justify their own faith, but fail miserably to do that honestly and logically!

Although Muslims express their belief in all the previous Scriptures (Tawraat, Zaboor and Injeel=The Holy Bible) as God's word along with the Qur'an, yet in practice they treat only Qur'an as God's (Allah's) word.

According to the Islamic sources called *Hadiths* (traditions) Qur'an is the compilation of the Arabic recitations that were given by the Islamic prophet Muhammad periodically, which he supposedly received from the angel Gabriel sent from Allah, in the early seventh century. These recitations were originally recorded on various materials such as bones, leaves, stones etc., which no longer exist today, and partly memorized by several of Muhammad's followers in a span of 22 years (610 AD–632 AD).

After Muhammad's death, these recorded recitations were supposedly collected and codified into one book, initially by one of Muhammad's scribes Zaid ibn Thabit under Abu Bakr the first *Caliph* (Islamic ruler) during his reign (632-634 A.D.). This first official Quran doesn't exist today. Later, under Uthman the third Caliph (644-656 A.D.), Zaid prepared another official Quran which also doesn't exist today.

SUMMARY OF THE QUR'AN'S POSITION ON THE HOLY BIBLE

The following points are significant as they stand against Muslims in their attitude towards the Holy Bible (Tawraat, Zaboor and Injeel):

- Nowhere does the Qur'an instruct its followers to *reject the Bible* (Tawraat, Zaboor and Injeel), yet Muslims reject the Bible without any hesitation.
- Nowhere does the Qur'an teach that the Bible (Tawraat, Zabur and Injeel) is *corrupted in its textual form* and thus declaring it *unreliable*.
- In some places the Qur'an accuses only the Jews of misinterpreting or misrepresenting the previous Scriptures i.e. the Holy Bible, but not corrupting or changing the texts

of the Scripture in every place. (S. 2:75; 4:46; 5:13; 5:41)
- In reality the Qur'an asserts that the Tawraat, Zaboor and Injeel (the Holy Bible) are sent down from Allah and are Allah's word. (S. 5:43-47; 21:105)
- Qur'an even declares that Allah's words cannot be changed, yet Muslims disbelieve this assertion in the case of the Tawraat, Zabur and Injeel. This disbelief or even doubt makes Muslims commit a great *shirk* (blasphemy) about Allah's word. Those who commit this sin become *kufr* (unbeliever)! (S. 6:34, 115; 10:64; 15:9)
- Qur'an threatens with severest punishment anybody who dares to say negative things against the Tawraat, Zaboor and Injeel (the Holy Bible). (S. 40:70-72)
- Qur'an admonishes both Jews and Christians to follow the Bible (Tawraat, Zaboor and Injeel) which is impossible for Jews and Christians to obey if their Bible is changed and unreliable as Muslims falsely accuse. Here too Muslims go against the Qur'an and its assertions and thereby commit *shirk*. (S. 5:43, 47)
- The Qur'an even teaches Muslims to believe and treat the Bible (Tawraat, Zaboor and Injeel) as they treat the Qur'an. But sadly Muslims pay no attention to this instruction and thus they are guilty before the Quranic Allah. (S. 3:84)
- What's more, the Qur'an advises the Islamic prophet Muhammad to consult Jews and Christians if he is in doubt about God's revelations for they have God's word (Tawraat, Zaboor and Injeel) with them, but Muslims totally fail in following their prophet in this most important example he set before them. Again, this also makes them guilty before Allah that brings punishment on them. (S. 32:23; 10:94)

AN INTERACTION WITH A MUSLIM

In 1998 I happened to sit next to a pious Muslim man on a small domestic plane in a Muslim dominated country. While we were flying when his time of prayer (*Namaaz*) had come he did manage to offer it in the air even in that extremely limited space that was available to any single person on that little forty-passenger plane.

Soon after finishing his religious obligation we both had an interesting exchange of religious convictions. During our low-voice exchanges my fellow Muslim passenger told me that my Bible that contains the Tawraat, Zaboor and Injeel is no longer pure and reliable. By making that outrageous statement he appeared as if he were going to establish the grounds for his faith up against mine. Unfortunately, his statement gave way for me to make him scramble for shelter under excuses. Our interaction went something like below:

Muhammad: The Bible which is basically the Tawraat, Zaboor and Injeel was actually given by Allah to Jews and Christians. But now it is corrupted and therefore not reliable. That is why Allah gave the Qur'an.
Abdul Rub: That's very interesting. May I ask you some questions about this statement you've just made?
Muhammad: No problem. Go ahead.
Abdul Rub: You believe that the Tawraat, Zaboor and Injeel were given by Allah, right?
Muhammad: That's correct. But not in their current form. Because they all got corrupted by Jews and Christians.
Abdul Rub: Oh I see! Have you read any one of those three books?
Muhammad: No, of course not. They are corrupted; why should I read them?
Abdul Rub: Wow! This is fascinating. You believe that the Tawraat, Zaboor and Injeel were from Allah, but without even reading them you hold them as corrupted! For example, if I say to you, 'I have never read the Quran but I tell you that it is a false book and not from God.' How would you feel? Would you accept that from me?
Muhammad: No, no. I can't accept that. How can you tell without even reading it? First you need to read it and then you will know the truth about it.
Abdul Rub: That's correct. The same is what I am telling you to do. First read the Injeel before telling lies about it.

ARGUMENT FROM WILD-GUESSES

If Muslims take the stand to accuse the Bible (the Tawraat, Zaboor and Injeel) of corruption ignoring the Qur'an's warnings against such evil accusations, that only shows their rational bankruptcy. If they were true in their accusation, then they should be able to answer the following questions not just with wild guesses and assumptions, but with corroborative evidence from historical sources:

a. Who corrupted? Christians or Jews? Since these two groups don't agree about God's word, how did they come to agree to such an evil thing without spilling the beans?
b. When was it corrupted? Before or after Muhammad? If it was before Muhammad, why then did Muhammad himself promote it without branding it as a corrupted book? If it was after Muhammad, how can it be possible for all the thousands of the ancient manuscripts to become corrupt in the same parts while they were located all over the Middle East in the hands of different people?
c. Why was it corrupted? Who would benefit from the corruption? What was the benefit of the corruption?
d. Where did it happen? Which place and under whose authority or collusion did it happen?
e. Why doesn't even a single so-called uncorrupted copy out of thousands of the ancient extant manuscripts exist today?

However, if Muslims still prefer to believe that the Bible *viz.* the Tawraat, Zaboor and Injeel, as originally given doesn't exist even in parts, then they are guilty of declaring that Allah who gave the Tawraat, Zaboor and Injeel failed miserably to protect them from being lost while the human-authored books of the Jewish and Christians Scriptures survived to this day. This makes Allah's power inferior to that of human authors! In the light of this truth Muslims should answer why anyone would believe in such a weak Allah!

INCONSISTENT BELIEF

Muslims claim that they believe what Allah said. Based on that belief they also believe that the Qur'an is preserved by Allah as he assured its preservation in the Qur'an. Nonetheless, in the same breath they make Allah a liar by disbelieving and ignoring what Allah said about his words in the Quran (S. 6:34, 115; 10:64; 15:9

cf. S. 5:43-47; 21:105). They also ignore what Allah (God) said in the Tawraat, Zaboor and Injeel about their preservation (Psalm 19:7, 119:89; Isiah 30:8, 40:8; Mat.5:18; Lk.21:33; Heb.2:2; 1Pet.1:25).

This blasphemous approach of Muslims in general to Allah's words prompted my brother in Christ Kamal and his wife - both are from Afghanistan - to find out the truth for themselves at any cost even by searching for it in the previous Scriptures. Despite the threats from their own family members to disown them as well as receiving death threats from the people around them they resolutely pressed on in search of the truth and found it. Of course, for that noble reason they had to count the cost by fleeing their homeland Afghanistan.

LOGICAL IMPOSSIBILITY

Muslims, apart from committing *shirk* (blasphemy) blindly reject Allah's power and truthfulness in protecting the Tawraat, Zaboor and Injeel despite Allah declaring that no one can change his words and his word would abide forever (S. 6:34, 115; 10:64; 15:9). While denying Allah's protecting power to some of His words (Tawraat, Zaboor and Injeel) Muslims irrationally believe that Allah has protected only the Qur'an, which is one of the four books Allah supposedly gave. This makes the Islamic Allah imperfect in his power, to say the least, for he could not protect all the books he sent down!

As a matter of fact, Allah gave the promise of preservation in his first three books. But Muslim believe in spite of that promise those books got corrupted. If this were the case, then how could they believe this Allah, who failed to keep his promise in the case of the first three books, to keep his promise in the case of the fourth book?

The truth of God was revealed and established by several inspired men of God, starting from prophet Moses, in the form of the Jewish Scriptures. The same truth of God has been properly interpreted, expanded, fulfilled and completed, again, by several inspired men of God in the form of the Christian Scriptures that heralded the end of God's Scriptural revelations.

If God's truth were to be corrected and reestablished by one-man revelations or religions, not only Islam fits the bill the Bahai religion, Mormonism, the Ahmadiya religion, Russellism etc. would also claim legitimacy of their religions in their own right. This would open the door for endless new religious initiatives among mankind as time progresses.

Finally, if Muslims think that the Qur'an made the Bible obsolete and thus abrogated it why then the Islamic prophet Muhammad never said anything to that effect? Instead, he supposedly gave the revelation that insists both Jews and Christians should be judged by the Scriptures given to them. Elsewhere in the Qur'an he even admonishes Jews and Christians that they must follow the Scriptures given to them (S.5:43,47). These facts from the Qur'an confirm Muhammad himself never believed that the previous Scriptures were canceled and became irrelevant.

TEXTUAL CRITICISM

Muslims are fond of quoting liberal theologians or atheistic critics of the Bible to justify their fallacious belief that the Bible is changed or corrupted. But, they never venture to apply the same criticism and criterion to the Qur'an!

Bart Erhman is one of the often quoted anti-Bible scholars by the Muslim apologists in their case against the Bible. Bart Erhman doesn't believe in God, the inspired word of God, miracles, Jesus' virgin birth etc. With this position, the same anti-Bible scholar is also anti-Qur'an. Yet, Muslims appeal to his opinions as dictum, however, only with regard to the authenticity of the Bible, but not the Qur'an. This is just one of the countless instances where the Muslim apologists commit the fallacy of double standard. This way any false religion can be 'proved to be true!'

As far as the science of the Textual Criticism is concerned both the Bible and the Qur'an fare well, although the Bible stands on a much higher moral ground than the Qur'an in this area. If Muslims think that the existence of the variant readings in the ancient manuscripts extant is the reason enough to reject the

The Holy Bible: Muslim Objections and Christian Responses

Bible as God's word, by the same token the Qur'an also should be rejected as God's word by Muslims.

INTERACTING WITH MUSLIMS

In my personal conversations and discussions with Muslims I make the following statements as the Christian premises and give them questions that follow them in order to elicit their stand with regard to the preservation of God's word:

Statement1: God exists!
Statement2: God spoke to mankind.
Statement3: God caused His speech/words to be recorded for mankind.
Statement4: God cannot fail to protect His written speech/words for mankind till the end.

After making the above statements I give them the following questions in a spirit of love and respect:

Question1: Does Allah exist?
Question2: If He does, had Allah spoken to mankind before He gave the Quran?
Question2: If so, did Allah make His speech/words to be written down as Tawraat, Zaboor and Injeel?
Question3: If yes, did or can Allah fail to protect His speech/words – Tawraat, Zaboor and Injeel – till the end?

These questions usually force the Muslims I converse with to face and realize their fallacious assumptions in labeling the Bible as changed or corrupted or lost. Of course, some of them might prefer to say 'yes' to the first three questions and 'no' to the fourth question and then try to tell us that the Bible is not the Tawraat, Zaboor and Injeel that Allah had given before the Quran. In which case, I insist on knowing where those books that Allah had given before the Quran are now. If they are honest enough this will enable them to see and realize the final fallacy in their position with regard to the Bible.

4. CHRISTIAN POSITION ON THE QUR'AN

Muslims in general take it for granted that the Qur'an is truly from Allah without any critical thinking or examination. One autumn evening in 2001 I was traveling in a public taxi with few others in a Muslim area. One of my fellow travelers was an elderly Muslim lady who told me passionately that the Qur'an was thrown out of heaven, literally, from Allah and therefore it is the true book of Allah! Blind beliefs like this gave rise to countless number of superstitious beliefs among Muslims regarding the Qur'an. If this can happen even in these modern days, how much more it had happened in the years following the Islamic prophet Muhammad's death!

HADITH LITERATURE

The above example explains how hundreds of thousands of stories began to form among Muslims between the late seventh century and early ninth century in order to elevate the Muhammad of history to the Muhammad of traditions. It is believed that there are more than 700,000 stories formed within a period of 150 years after Muhammad's death. Muslim scholar Imam Al-Bukhari collected and examined around 600,000 of such stories in the middle of ninth century.

The traditions or stories regarding Muhammad that began to form and circulate among Muslims in the years following Muhammad's death are called 'Hadiths.' Each Hadith is a short story containing *matn* (text) of the story and *isnad* (chain of narrators). Every single Hadith invariably depicts either the sayings of Muhammad or his actions or his silence. The morals or examples enshrined in these stories form the perfect model for Muslims' life and hope.

Islamic history (*tariq*), Muhammad's biography (*sira*) and Qur'an's interpretations (*tafsir*) all come from the Hadith literature.

What is Islam, how and when was it started? The answer is in the Hadith literature.

What are the essential beliefs and practices of Islam and how to follow it? The answer is in the Hadith literature.

Who is the Islamic prophet Muhammad? The answer is in the Hadith literature.

What is the Qur'an and how did it come? The answer is in the Hadith literature.

What are the contexts of the Qur'anic revelations? The answer is in the Hadith literature.

What is the interpretation of the Qur'anic verses? The answer is in the Hadith literature.

In short, it is the Hadith literature that forms the foundation as well as building of Islam.

From his studies of the Hadith literature Al-Bukhari declared only 7,295 Hadiths are authentic and the rest – 99% - are spurious based on a set of criteria that he developed. These so-called authentic Hadith stories have been codified as Sahih Hadiths. There are a few other Muslim scholars who did the same at later stages examining popular stories and codifying some of them into Hadiths. One of Al-Bukhari's disciples by the name Muslim was another scholar who separated the so-called authentic Hadiths from the spurious ones.

The Hadith literature is broadly divided into three groups. *Sahih* Hadiths (considered as authentic), *Hasan* Hadiths (considered as reliable) and *Daif* Hadiths (considered as weak).

The following are a few examples of the authentic or Sahih Hadiths collected and codified by Bukhari and Muslim:

Example#1:

"Narrated Abu Huraira:

The Prophet said "If a house fly falls in the drink of anyone of you, he should dip it (in the drink), for one of its wings has a disease and the other has the cure for the disease." (*Sahih Al-Bukhari*: Volume 4, Book 54, Number 537)

Example#2:

"Narrated by Anas

When 'Abdullah bin Salam heard the arrival of the Prophet at Medina, he came to him and said, "I am going to ask you about three things which nobody knows except a prophet: What is the first portent of the Hour? What will be the first meal taken by the people of Paradise? Why does a child resemble its father, and why does it resemble its maternal uncle" Allah's Apostle said, "Gabriel has just now told me of their answers." 'Abdullah said, "He (i.e. Gabriel), from amongst all the angels, is the enemy of the Jews." Allah's Apostle said, "The first portent of the Hour will be a fire that will bring together the people from the east to the west; the first meal of the people of Paradise will be Extra-lobe (caudate lobe) of fish-liver. As for the resemblance of the child to its parents: If a man has sexual intercourse with his wife and gets discharge first, the child will resemble the father, and if the woman gets discharge first, the child will resemble her." On that 'Abdullah bin Salam said, "I testify that you are the Apostle of Allah."...(*Sahih Al-Bukhari*: Volume 4, Book 55, Number 546)

Example#3:

"It is narrated on the authority of Abu Dharr that the Messenger of Allah (may peace be upon him) one day said: Do you know where the sun goes? They replied: Allah and His Apostle know best. He (the Holy Prophet) observed: Verily it (the sun) glides till it reaches its resting place under the Throne. Then it falls prostrate and remains there until it is asked: Rise up and go to the place whence you came, and it goes back and continues emerging out from its rising place and then glides till it reaches its place of rest under the Throne and falls prostrate and remains in that state until it is asked: Rise up and return to the place whence you came, and it returns and emerges out from it rising place and the it glides (in such a normal way) that the people do not discern anything (unusual in it) till it reaches its resting place under the Throne. Then it would be said to it: Rise up and emerge out from the place of your setting, and it will rise from the place of its setting. The Messenger of Allah (may peace be upon him) said. Do you know when it would happen? It would happen at the time when faith will not benefit one who has not previously believed or has derived no good from the faith." (*Sahih Muslim*, Book 1, Hadith Number 297)

Example#4

> Abu Huraira reported: The Apostle of Allah said. When any one of you awakes up from sleep and performs ablution, he must clean his nose three times, for the devil spends the night in the interior of his nose. (*Sahih Muslim*, Book 002, Number 0462)

The problem with these 'wise' and 'enlightening' stories is self-evident. Although the contents of a significant number of the Hadith stories defy commonsense and fly in the face of all reason they do shape the morale, confidence, convictions and practices of Muslims.

Hadiths like the above form the basis of the Islamic faith, practice, experience and hope. For instance, Muslims are required to offer prayers (*namaaz*) 'five times' a day which is one of the 'five pillars of Islam.' Yet, this important religious mandate for Muslims cannot be found in the Qur'an, but in the Hadith literature. *Khitan* or *Khatna* (circumcision) is another religious requirement for Muslim males. Again, this is also not in the Quran, but Hadiths. Hadiths also provide context, chronology, clarity, history and authenticity for the Qur'an as Allah's word. This simply does not go well with objective thinkers and honest truth seekers.

Apart from the fact that the codification, reliability and contents of the Hadith literature are highly questionable, they do contain internal contradictions as well. Different sects in Islam - major sects such as Sunni, Shia, Sufi and minor sects numbering in several hundred if not thousands - chose different sets of Hadiths to base their ideologies and ritual actions. Ironically, within the framework of the vast and conflicting corpus of Hadith literature all sects can claim legitimacy and yet be at each other's throats!

THE QUR'AN

Based on the Qur'anic verses, which in turn are based on the Hadith literature, Muslims believe that the Qur'an is also from the same God who sent the Tawraat, Zaboor and Injeel (the Holy Bible). This cannot be true from the Christian point of view for the following reasons:

(1) Completion of the Revelation: The Bible is the complete revelation of God to mankind, and the Injeel or the New Testament is the final and perfect revelation as a part of God's progressive revelation. It is sufficient for faith, practice, experience and hope. It addresses all the questions of concern to mankind. It's neither incomplete nor insufficient in terms of God's revelation to mankind. Therefore, there is no need for another book from God.

(2) Authentication: The true divine inspiration came through several chosen men of God in both prophetic lineage and Apostolic authority who authenticated one another (Josh.1:8; 1 Sam.12:6; Dan.9:2,12; Neh.13:1; Zech.7:12; Matt.4:4,7,10, 5:17-18, 22:29,43-44; Mk.9:12, 12:26; Lk.16:16,31, 24:44; Jn.10:34-35; 2Cor.13:3,10; Eph.3:1-6; 1Thess.2:13; 2Thess.2:13-15; 1Tim.5:18 = Duet.25:4+Lk.10:7; 2Tim.3:16; 1Pet.1:10-12; 2Pet.1:21, 3:1-2, 15-16; Rev.1:1-3, 9-19). Neither the Islamic prophet Muhammad nor the Qur'an he gave has this vital authentication. In fact, Muhammad neither belongs to the prophetic lineage nor has the Apostolic authority of the Judeo-Christian faith.

(3) Teachings: The Qur'an contains teachings that are both conflicting with and abhorrent to the teachings of the Bible.

i) Rituals associated with the Kaabah in Mecca: As one of the 'five pillars of Islam' it is mandatory for all adult Muslims, who are physically and financially capable of undertaking journey, to go for an 'annual pilgrimage to Mecca' (*Hajj*) at least once in lifetime. 8th to 12th of the last month (*Dhu al-Hijjah*) in the Islamic calendar Muslims from all over the world would converge in Mecca to perform various rituals in and around the *Kaaba*, which is a cubical structure that holds the pieces of a black stone in a silver container on one of its corners. The pilgrims would walk counter-clock wise around the Kaaba seven times and, if possible, kiss the Kaaba and the black stone, run back and forth between the hills *Al-Safa* and *Al-Marwah*, drink water from *Zamzam* well, go to the Mount *Arafat* to stand in vigil, spend a night in the plains of *Muzdalifa*, perform the symbolic stoning of the devil by throwing stones at three pillars, shave or trim their heads, participate in animal sacrifices, and in the end celebrate three days of *Eid al-Adha* festival.

From the eighth century onwards in an effort to justify the Hajj rituals Muslims began to claim that the above rituals were originally installed by the biblical prophets! Although the Qur'an itself doesn't make any reference to this claim Muslims make this claim based on the Hadith literature which has no historical basis at all in this regard. The truth is none of the Biblical prophets had ever started or participated in any of these rituals in Mecca. All the rituals including venerating the black stone in Kaabah are foreign to the Biblical prophets because they are abhorrent to the God of the Bible. In fact, quite a number of these ritual performances of Hajj were being practiced by the pre-Islamic Arab Pagans in Mecca before the Islamic religion was started in 610 A.D.

ii) Allah creates people for Hell: The Bible teaches that Hell is created for the devil and his followers, but it doesn't teach that the people are created for Hell (Matt.25:41)! The God of the Bible doesn't wish anyone to perish in Hell (1Tim.2:3-4). However, the Qur'an teaches otherwise:

"And surely, <u>We have created</u> many of the jinns and <u>mankind for Hell</u>. They have hearts wherewith they understand not, they have eyes wherewith they see not, and they have ears wherewith they hear not (the truth). They are like cattle, nay even more astray; those! They are the heedless ones." (S 7:178-179)

> "A'isha, the mother of the believers, said that Allah's Messenger was called to lead the funeral prayer of a child of the Ansar. I said: Allah's Messenger, there is happiness for this child who is a bird from the birds of Paradise for it committed no sin nor has he reached the age when one can commit sin.
> He said: 'A'isha, per adventure, it may be otherwise, because God created for Paradise those who are fit for it while they were yet in their father's loins <u>and created for Hell those who are to go to Hell. He created them for Hell while they were yet in their father's loins</u>." (*Sahih Muslim*, Book 033, Number 6436)

iii) Divorce and remarriage: The Bible teaches that a woman divorced by her husband can rejoin him if they both reconcile with each other. But if she marries another person after had been divorced by the first one she should not rejoin the first one in marriage for it is abominable in the sight of God (Deut.24:1-4).

However, the Qur'an teaches the opposite:

"So if a husband divorces his wife (irrevocably), He cannot, after that, remarry her until after she has married another husband and He has divorced her. In that case there is no blame on either of them if they re-unite, provided they feel that they can keep the limits ordained by God. Such are the limits ordained by God, which He makes plain to those who understand." (S 2:230)

iv) Women's status as opposed to men: The Bible teaches that both man and woman are created in the image of God and are appointed as the rulers of the rest of the creation (Gen.1:27-28, 5:1-2, 9:6; Jam.3:9). Though they differ in their anatomy and strengths, due to which they assume different roles in this world, yet there is no essential difference between their worth and destiny (Matt.22:30; Gal.3:28; 1Pet.3:7). But the teachings of the Qur'an and Hadiths go completely opposite to the Biblical teachings.

*"…But if he who oweth the debt is of low understanding, or weak, or unable himself to dictate, then let the guardian of his interests dictate in (terms of) equity. And call to witness, from among your men, two witnesses. And if two men be not (at hand) then a man and **two women**, of such as ye approve as witnesses, so that if the one erreth (through forgetfulness) the other will remember…"* (S 2:282)

> Narrated Abu Said Al-Khudri: "The Prophet said, "Isn't the witness of a woman equal to half of that of a man?" The women said, "Yes." He said, "This is because of the deficiency of a woman's mind." (*Sahih Bukhari*, Volume 3, Book 48, Number 826)

*"Men are in charge of women, because Allah hath made the one of them to excel the other, and because they spend of their property (for the support of women). So good women are the obedient, guarding in secret that which Allah hath guarded. As for those from whom ye **fear** rebellion, admonish them and banish them to beds apart, and **scourge** them. Then if they obey you, seek not a way against them. Lo! Allah is ever High, Exalted, Great."* (S 4:34)

"*Your wives are as a <u>tilth unto you</u>; so <u>approach your tilth when or how ye will</u>; but do some good act for your souls beforehand; and fear God. And know that ye are to meet Him (in the Hereafter), and give (these) good tidings to those who believe.*" (S 2:223)

In the following Hadiths the Islamic prophet Muhammad equates women with animals such as ass, dog and horse:

> Abu Dharr reported: <u>The Messenger of Allah</u> (may peace be upon him) <u>said</u>: When any one of you stands for prayer and there is a thing before him equal to the back of the saddle that covers him and in case there is not before him (a thing) equal to the back of the saddle, his prayer would be cut off by (passing of an) <u>ass, **woman**, and black dog</u>. I said: O Abu Dharr, what feature is there in a black dog which distinguish it from the red dog and the yellow dog? He said: O, son of my brother, I asked the <u>Messenger of Allah</u> (may peace be upon him) as you are asking me, and <u>he said: The black dog is a devil</u>. (*Sahih Muslim*, Book 004, Number 1032)
> Narrated Abdullah bin 'Umar: Allah's Apostle said, "<u>Evil omen is in the **women**, the house and the horse.</u>" (*Sahih al-Bukhari*, Volume 7, Book 62, Number 30, 31,32)

(4) Relationship with others: The final teachings of the Bible as found in the Injeel or the New Testament form the greatest standard for all mankind till the end. On the contrary, the teachings of Qur'an are of substandard nature in comparison to the teachings of the Injeel with regard to the attitude towards others—neighbors and enemies.

The Injeel (The New Testament):
- "*So in everything, **do to others** what **you would have them do to you**, for this sums up the Law and the Prophets.*" (Matt.7:12)
- "<u>*love your neighbor* **as yourself**</u>". (Matt.19:19)
- "*But I tell you, **love your enemies** and **pray** for those who **persecute you**"* (Matt.5:44)

The Qur'an:

- "*Serve God, and join not any partners with Him; and **do good*** - *to parents, kinsfolk, orphans, those in need, <u>neighbours who are near, neighbours who are strangers</u>, the companion by your side, <u>the wayfarer</u> (ye meet), and*

what your right hands possess: For God loveth not the arrogant, the vainglorious" (S 4:36)
- *"The forbidden month for the forbidden month, and forbidden things in retaliation. And <u>one who attacketh you, attack him in like manner as he attacked you</u>. Observe your duty to Allah, and know that Allah is with those who ward off (evil)."* (S 2:194)
- *"Then, when the sacred months have passed, <u>slay the idolaters wherever ye find them, and take them (captive), and besiege them, and prepare for them each ambush</u>. But if they repent and establish worship and pay the poor-due, then leave their way free. Lo! Allah is Forgiving, Merciful."* (S 9:5)
- *"<u>Fight</u> those who believe not in God nor the Last Day, nor hold that forbidden which hath been forbidden by God and His Apostle, nor acknowledge the religion of Truth, (even if they are) of the People of the Book, <u>until they pay the Jizya with willing submission, and feel themselves subdued</u>."* (S 9:29)

Of course, Muslim apologists try to explain the above verses away by saying that these verses were given in the seventh century war contexts and are therefore not commands to follow these days or in other than similar war situations. This explanation creates more problems for the Muslim apologists than the solution they hope for the following reasons:

- The Qur'an itself doesn't mention or offer any context and time that have been suggested by the Muslim apologists.
- Even if one were to accept the Muslim apologists' explanation one is left with no concrete and reliable source that provides the context and time of these verses.
- If the Muslim apologists' explanation is correct in the case of these verses, then the Muslim belief that the Qur'an as a whole is Allah's eternal speech turns out to be false.
- If the Muslim apologists' explanation is correct, then the Muslim belief that the Qur'an is perfect and complete is also false for it lacks important information such as contexts and times of its teachings.
- Finally, if the Muslim apologists' explanation is correct, then

the true meaning of the Qur'an depends on human information coming from outside of Allah's direct speech. This, of course, confirms that the Qur'an is incomplete, imperfect, dependent and not eternal!

There is another 'answer' Muslim apologists try to offer in their futile attempts to prove that the Qur'an is not a book that advocates violence but upholds sanctity of all lives. In this effort they quote the following verse from the Qur'an:

"Whosoever killeth a human being for other than manslaughter or corruption in the earth, it shall be as if he had killed all mankind, and whoso saveth the life of one, it shall be as if he had saved the life of all mankind." (S.5:32)

On its face value the above verse appears very appealing to and justifying the Muslim apologists' position on the Qur'anic 'noble' teaching. However, if we read the whole verse in its context the deception employed by the Muslim apologists becomes obvious and their hypocritical approach will be exposed for all to see. Here is the same verse in its entirety:

"For that cause <u>We decreed for the Children of Israel</u> that *whosoever killeth a human being for other than manslaughter or corruption in the earth, it shall be as if he had killed all mankind, and whoso saveth the life of one, it shall be as if he had saved the life of all mankind.* **Our messengers came unto them of old with clear proofs (of Allah's Sovereignty), but afterwards lo! many of them became prodigals in the earth."** (S.5:32)

From the above verse now we can see that the noble teaching on the sanctity of life was decreed for the Children of Israel, not Muslims, as the verse itself testifies to. As a matter of fact, this particular teaching is taken from the commentaries of the Jewish scholars or Rabbis on Torah (Pentateuch) in reference to Genesis 4:10 where Cain's murder of his brother Abel is mentioned. In reference to this incident the Jewish Rabbis made the following comment in Talmud:

"Therefore the man was created singly, to teach that he who destroys one soul of a human being, the Scripture considers him as if he should destroy a whole world, and him who saves one soul of Israel, the Scripture considers him as if he should save a whole world." (Talmud, *Tractate Sanhedrin*, Chapter 4)

The Talmudic commentaries - including the noble teaching the Qur'an mentions in surah 5:32 - were produced in 200 A.D., that is, 400 years before the Qur'an was written down. The obvious conclusion is that Muhammad mistook the Talmudic commentaries that were being used by the Jews of his time in Hijaz to be God's word and therefore quoted it in surah 5:32.

(5) Personal Name of God: Jewish as well as Christian Scriptures were given through the divinely inspired men of God who knew and professed the personal name of the true God 'YHWH' (YaHWeH) as given by God Himself to prophet Moses (Ex.3:13-15). But none of the revelations in the Qur'an were given in the personal name of the true God i.e. 'YHWH' (YaHWeH), or by those who knew and professed that name. Knowledge of and allegiance to this divine name becomes all the more indispensable when any so-called Scripture or prophet from other than Jewish national, religious or cultural background seeks to claim coming from the God of Moses who gave His personal name in categorical terms.

(6) Moral problem: The Bible exposes the wickedness of mankind. It doesn't shield even the prophets or priests or princes when they sin against their neighbours and against God. King

David was exposed and punished for his lust towards his neighbour's wife (1Sam.11:1-2:15). However, the way Qur'an deals with a private and lone encounter of the Islamic prophet Muhammad with Zaynab, his adopted son Zaid's wife. The subsequent divorce of Zaynab by Zaid on the heels of which came Muhammad's marriage with Zaynab is morally troubling if not abhorring even by the standards of that time (S. 33:37).

(7) Mathematical problem: With regard to inheritance law the Qur'an gives instructions that are impossible to follow in some cases. The following are the Qur'anic instructions on 'inheritance law':

"God (thus) directs you as regards your Children's (Inheritance): <u>to the male, a portion equal to that of two females</u>: if only daughters, two or more, their share is two-thirds of the inheritance; if only one, her share is a half. For parents, a sixth <u>share of the inheritance</u> to each, if the deceased left children; if no children, and the parents are the (only) heirs, the mother has a third; if the deceased Left brothers (or sisters) the mother has a sixth. (The distribution in all cases ('s) after the payment of legacies and debts. Ye know not whether your parents or your children are nearest to you in benefit. These are settled portions ordained by God; and God is All-knowing, Al-wise. (S 4:11)

"In what your wives leave, your share is a half, if they leave no child; but if they leave a child, ye get a fourth; after payment of legacies and debts. <u>In what ye leave</u>, their share is a fourth, if ye leave no child; but if ye leave a child, they get an eighth; after payment of legacies and debts. If the man or woman whose inheritance is in question, has left neither ascendants nor descendants, but has left a brother or a sister, each one of the two gets a sixth; but if more than two, they share in a third; after payment of legacies and debts; so that no loss is caused (to any one). Thus is it ordained by God; and God is All-knowing, Most Forbearing." (S 4:12)

Let's try to follow the above instructions in three different scenarios as given below:

Scenario#1: A man died leaving a son, a daughter, one parent and one wife behind. If we divide his wealth according to the above instructions we get (the available total shares is 1):

Share of one parent	Share of one wife	Remainder of the inheritance	Share of one son	Share of one daughter	Total Shares must be equal to the inheritance
1/6th of the inheritance (assuming the total inheritance being 1 unit) According to S.4:11	1/8th of the inheritance (assuming the total inheritance being 1 unit) According to S.4:12	1-(7/24)= 0.708333 3unit.	2/3rd of the remaining inheritance (0.7083333 unit) According to S.4:11	1/3rd of the remaining inheritance (0.7083333unit) According to S.4:11	2/3+1/3=1 i.e. 0.7083333unit = 0.7083333 which is the remainder of the inheritance

(The distribution can be done in two stages due to the phrases *'to the male, a portion equal to that of two females'* with regard to son and daughter, and *'of the inheritance to each'* with regard to parent and wife)

The result is perfect!

Scenario#2: A man died leaving three daughters, one parent and one wife behind. If we try to divide his wealth according to the above Qur'anic instructions we get:

Share of 3 daughters	Share of 1 parent	Share of 1 wife	Total shares must be equal to the inheritance
2/3rd of the total inheritance (assuming the total inheritance being 1 unit) According to S.4:11	1/6th of the inheritance (assuming the total inheritance being 1 unit) According to S.4:11	1/8th of the inheritance (assuming the total inheritance being 1 unit) According to S.4:12	2/3+1/6+1/8=0.9583 unit. Unclaimed parts of the inheritance = 0.0417unit!

(Because of the phrases *'of the inheritance'* with regard to the daughters, and *'In what ye leave'* with regard to the parent and wife we cannot do the above distribution in two stages like in the first case.)

The result is a bit problematic. What do we do with the remaining inheritance? Why didn't the Islamic Allah provide some instructions about that too in the Qur'an?

Scenario#3: A man died leaving three daughters, two parents and one wife behind. If we try to divide his wealth according to the Qur'anic instructions we get:

Share of 3 daughters	Share of 2 parents	Share of 1 wife	Total inheritance must be equal to the inheritance
2/3rd of the inheritance (assuming the total inheritance being 1 unit) According to S.4:11	1/3rd of the inheritance (assuming the total inheritance being 1 unit) According to S.4:11	1/8th of the inheritance (assuming the total inheritance being 1 unit) According to S.4:12	2/3+1/3+1/8=1.125 units. Extra needed to be given to the inheritors = 0.125! Who gives this?

(Because of the phrases *'of the inheritance'* and *'In what ye leave'* we cannot do the above distribution in two stages like in the first case)

The result is shocking!

The Qur'anic Allah's instructions are based on erroneous calculations to say the least. If we follow them they lead us to wrong conclusions. Where do we get the extra inheritance i.e. 0.125, for the distribution? This is why in real life situations even Muslims ignore these imperfect instructions given in the Qur'an in order to get the appropriate shares of their inheritances. In reality, they turn to human traditions and decisions that can do their job properly for they are far more helpful and wiser than the Qur'anic instructions.

Does the true God make these mathematical blunders in His instructions? Would the All-knowing God ever give this kind of imperfect instructions that would cause unimaginable confusion to those who faithfully seek to implement the above Qur'anic instructions? Never! But that is exactly what the Qur'an proposes. That is why the Qur'an is not from the true God.

(8) Heavenly reward: The Qur'an promises to its believers a Heaven that is meant to satisfy the carnal pleasures. According to the Qur'an believers will be ushered into a Paradise where there are rivers of honey, milk and wine to enjoy. Apart from these drinking pleasures they will be **wedded** to beautiful heavenly girls called *huris* (S. 47:15; 55:56-58; 78:32-34). The number of *huris* one gets in the Islamic Paradise and the graphic description of the beauty of *huris* are given in the Hadith literature. This is in direct contradiction to the concept of Heaven in the Judeo-Christian Scriptures. The Bible rules out any carnal pleasure such as sexual relations, drinking wine etc. It's a place of God's presence where the faithful enjoy eternal life without hunger, thirst, pain, suffering and sexual needs. (Is.49:10; Mak.12:23-25; Rev.21:3-4)

(9) Influence: On a verifiable front we can see in today's world there are those who emulate peace, love, forgiveness, tolerance and charity, and then there are those who try to emulate violence, hate, tit-for-tat attitude, intolerance to minorities and suicide bombings etc. Such actions generally be traced either to the teachings of the Injeel or Qur'an. Christians cannot help but see the conspicuous fruits of each book, the Injeel and Qur'an, which also confirm to them that the Qur'an cannot be from God.

(10) Status of transgender: The author of the Qur'an makes the bold statement that Allah created everything in pairs!

"*And* **of everything** *We have created pairs: That ye may receive instruction.*" (S.51:49)

A claim about 'everything' is an extraordinary claim. Only God as the omniscient Being can make claims about everything. If a false god or a mere human falsely claiming to speak for God makes a claim about everything, it is very easy to find that out – by finding something that contradicts the claim!

The above claim gives us the clue to know if the Qur'an is truly from God. Unlike in the seventh century Arabia now it has been discovered that quite a number of living things do not have pairs. The following are some examples that have only one gender or both genders, but without a pair!

Living organism, insects and plants: Bacteria; single cell organism amoeba; parthenogenetics—invertebrates and lower plants; bdelloid rotifers; Bees; cnemidophoras lizards; aphids etc.
Human beings: Naturally born eunuchs or transgender persons!

The other problem that the claim in the Qur'an exposes is the total failure to recognize and give the asexual persons any concern, value or hope by the author of the Qur'an. In contrast, the God of the Bible not only recognizes the asexual persons but also affirms their value by providing them a blessed hope:

"And let no eunuch complain, "I am only a dry tree." For this is what the LORD says: "To the eunuchs who keep my Sabbaths, who choose what pleases me and hold fast to my covenant—to them I will give within my temple and its walls a memorial and a name better than sons and daughters; I will give them an everlasting name that will endure forever." (Isaiah 56:3-5) NIV

(11) We are forewarned: Finally, we are clearly forewarned in the Bible regarding the false revelations, false religions and false representatives claiming to come from God. (cf.Matt.7:13-20, 24:11,24-26; Acts 20:28-30; 2Cor.11:14-15; 1Tim.4:1-5; 2Pet.2:1-3)

DOUBLE STANDARD

The Muslims who accuse the Bible of contradictions, errors, changes etc. have employed - knowingly or unknowingly - a double standard in judging the Bible which amounts to hypocrisy. Now we will see how the Qur'an fares if the same accusations and standard are applied to its contents.

For a non-Muslim the contents of the Quran pose insurmountable problems in the light of science, history and logic. But for Christians these problems are not the main reason why the Quran is considered as not from the one true God. The main reasons why Christians reject the Quran have already been laid out in the previous section. We shall now look at a few examples that demonstrate the point that Muslims tend to argue inconsistently and hypocritically against the Holy Bile while their own Quran is mired in similar problems. It is no surprise that Muslim scholars are at pains to justify the problems of the Quran and try to explain them away in irrational and inconsistent ways, albeit with little success in convincing honest thinkers.

The Qur'an claims that there are no discrepancies in it: *"Do they not consider the Qur'an? Had it been from other Than God, they would surely have found therein much discrepancy."* (Sura 4:82)

Let's see below if this claim is true. To make bold claims before seventh century illiterate Arabs is one thing and to back up those claims with convincing evidence is quite another thing!

Scientific problem # 1:

"And thy Lord inspired <u>the bee</u>, saying: Choose thou habitations in the hills and in the trees and in that which they thatch; <u>Then eat of all fruits</u>, and follow the ways of thy Lord, made smooth (for thee). There cometh forth from their bellies a drink divers of hues, wherein is healing for mankind. Lo! herein is indeed a portent for people who reflect." (Sura 16:68-69)

Obviously bees do not 'eat' of all fruits! Bees suck/drink the nectar from flowers. This is completely missing in the Qur'anic verse. Instead, the Qur'an enlightens its readers by teaching them that the bees were inspired to 'eat of all fruits!' The error of this verse is there for all to see.

Scientific problem # 2:

Qur'an teaches that the sky is solid!

"Allah it is Who <u>raised up the heavens</u> without visible supports..." (S. 13:2)

"Hast thou not seen how Allah hath made all that is in the earth subservient unto you? And the ship runneth upon the sea by His command, and <u>He holdeth back the heaven from falling on the earth</u> unless by His leave. Lo! Allah is, for mankind, Full of Pity, Merciful." (S. 22:65)

The above teaching of the Qur'an regarding the nature of the heaven i.e. sky, is anything but scientifically accurate.

Scientific problem # 3:

Allah created man from a clot of blood!

*"Proclaim! (or read!) in the name of thy Lord and Cherisher, <u>Who created - Created man,</u> **out of** a (mere) <u>clot of congealed blood</u>."* (S. 96:1-2)

Neither the creation of the first man Adam nor the creation of the subsequent human beings through procreation nor even the birth of test-tube babies through modern day invention fits this description.

The Qur'an says, '...created man out of a clot of blood!' However, it doesn't say, '...created man out of something that looks like a clot of blood!' or '...created man in the process with something that looks like a clot of blood!' Since blood (not blood clot) enters the picture of a growing fetus in the womb only in the fourth week after conception, the Quran is clearly in scientific error.

Scientific problem # 4:

Allah created seven earths!

"God is He Who created seven Firmaments and of the earth a similar number. Through the midst of them (all) descends His Command: that ye may know that God has power over all things, and that God comprehends, all things in (His) Knowledge." (S. 65:12)

This is clearly a false assertion.

Historic problem # 1:

Qur'an mixes up Mary (Arabic: Mariam) the mother of Jesus with Miriam (Hebrew: Mariam) the sister of Moses and Aaron. That is why it mentions Mary as the sister of Aaron and the daughter of Imran (19:28; 66:12)! Moses, Aaron and Miriam were the children of Amram (Arabic: Imran) and Jochebed who lived around 1500 BC.

Furthermore, Mary mother of Jesus was from the tribe of Judah and Miriam the sister of Aaron was from the tribe of Levi. But the Qur'an says that Mary had a brother whose name is Aaron (S 19:29) and a father whose name is Imran (S 66:12). Their mother is called wife of Imran (S 3:35). The error is obvious!

Historic problem # 2:

Qur'an reports that Pharaoh threatened to crucify people during Moses' time i.e. 1400 B.C. But the method of crucifixion was not even in use at that time. According to history it was in use between 600 B.C. to 400 A.D.

"Surely I shall have your hands and feet cut off upon alternate sides. Then I shall crucify you every one." (S 7:124)

The Encyclopedia Americana, Volume 8, 2000 edition, p. 260 states this:

> History of Crucifixion as Capital Punishment. Crucifixion was used as a form of capital punishment from about the 6th century B.C. to the 4th century A.D. It probably originated among the Persians, from whom it spread to other peoples such as the EGYPTIANS, Carthaginians, and Romans. Crucifixion was not inflicted on Roman citizens, but only on slaves and subject peoples. In 337, it was banned by Constantine the Great out of respect for Jesus Christ, who suffered death on the cross at the hands of the Roman rulers of Palestine.

Historic problem # 3:

"And the Jews say: 'Uzair (Ezra) is the son of Allah, and the Christians say: Messiah is the son of Allah. That is a saying from their mouths. They imitate the saying of the disbelievers of old. Allah's Curse be on them, how they are deluded away from the truth!" (S. 9:30)

In the above verse the author of the Qur'an accuses Christians that they say, 'Messiah is the son of Allah (God).' There is no doubt about this statement to some extent. Christians do believe that Jesus is the Son of God (Allah), not only during Muhammad's time but even today. However, not in physical sense - as the author of the Quran erroneously assumed - but in spiritual sense. In reality Jesus is the Son of God always, even before His birth in Bethlehem 2000 years ago. (cf. Prov.30:4; Jn.1:18, 3:16-17)

In the same verse the author accuses Jews that they say, 'Uzair (Ezra) is the son of Allah (God). This particular accusation is a false accusation as no Jew today believes that Uzair (Ezra) is the son of God (Allah). There is no historic record of any Jews anywhere ever calling Ezra (Uzair) the son of God (Allah), including during Muhammad's time. For argument sake even if we give the benefit of doubt to the Qur'an and assume that there might have been 'some' Jews who for some reason called Uzair (Ezra) the son of Allah (God) in Arabian peninsula during Muhammad's time, then the author should have said, 'And some Jews say: 'Uzair (Ezra) is the son of Allah.' Instead, the author says, '*And the Jews say: 'Uzair (Ezra) is the son of Allah,*' implying that all Jews of all times say that Uzair (Ezra) is the son of Allah (God). This is a clear historical mistake made by the author of the Qur'an.

Logical problem:

Moses introduced the law of retaliation as "*Show no pity: life for life, eye for eye, tooth for tooth, hand for hand, foot for foot*" in 1400 B.C. 1430 years later i.e. in 30 A.D., Jesus said, "*You have heard that it was said, 'Eye for eye, and tooth for tooth. But I tell you, do not resist an evil person.*" (Matt.5:38).

However, 580 years later i.e. in 620A.D., Muhammad gave the instruction, "*O ye who believe! Retaliation is prescribed for you in the matter of the murdered; <u>the freeman for the freeman, and the slave for the slave, and the female for the female</u>. And for him who is forgiven somewhat by his (injured) brother, <u>prosecution according to</u> usage and <u>payment</u> unto him in kindness. This is an alleviation and a mercy from your Lord. He who transgresseth after this will have a painful doom.*" (S 2:178)

(a) According to this verse of the Qur'an what are we supposed to make out from, 'the freeman for the freeman, and the slave for the slave, and the female for the female?' What's the logic of this sentence?

Does that mean if a free man is murdered by a slave of a free person, then for retaliation, the owner of that slave should be killed? Or if a slave of a person is murdered by a free person, then for retaliation the slave of the murderer should be killed? Or if a female person is killed by a male person, then for retaliation the wife of the murderer should be killed? Why not simply say "life for life, eye for eye, tooth for tooth?"

(b) There is another problem with this instruction. In what way would it be just if a murderer goes free by paying money (blood money) to a relative? This only implies that the verse is equating life of a person to money! Let's say if a near relative of a person arranged the murder of a person clandestinely, then the same relative who arranged the murder can easily and all too happily take money from the murderer he hired and grant him forgiveness.

Even in the case where the murder is not arranged, if the near relative is a greedy person, he could well take the money (blood money) without any respect to the person murdered or the end of justice. Isn't that strange? Hence there is no wisdom in this instruction. It rather causes gross miscarriage of justice and no civilized court in this world would operate such an instruction as meaningful and honorable. This instruction cannot be from the true God.

Clarity problem:

Qur'an makes a bold claim for itself.

Qur'an: Al-Qamar (The Moon) 54:17
"وَلَقَدْ يَسَّرْنَا الْقُرْآنَ لِلذِّكْرِ فَهَلْ مِن مُّدَّكِرٍ"
"*And We have indeed made the <u>Qur'an easy to understand and remember</u>: then is there any that will receive admonition?*"

But the reality is otherwise. The Qur'an lacks chronology, context, continuity and clarity. The Qur'an is frustratingly unclear, confusing and discontinuous. A first-time reader can testify to the fact that after reading the Qur'an without any external aids or information it feels like losing oneself in a sea of eccentric monologue.

Preservation problem:

Muslims believe that the Qur'an they have today is what Allah had sent through the angel Gabriel and revealed it to the Islamic prophet Muhammad in the early seventh century in the Arabian city called Mecca. According to the Islamic sources Muhammad in turn recited what he had received from the angel 'Gabriel' before his followers who wrote it down on various materials such as bones, leaves, stones etc. and also memorized them in parts. Later, it is the first Caliph Abu Bakr *ibn* (son of) Qhuhafah (632-634 A.D.) who ordered the scattered verses of the Qur'an to be compiled into one book. This Qur'an was first with Abu Bakr and then with Umar ibn Al-Khattab (second Caliph) and finally with Umar's daughter Hafsa who was one of the several wives Mohammad had. The following *Hadith* provides the story afterwards:

> "Narrated Anas bin Malik:
> Hudhaifa bin Al-Yaman came to Uthman at the time when the people of Sham and the people of Iraq were Waging war to conquer Arminya and Adharbijan. Hudhaifa was afraid of their (the people of Sham and Iraq) differences in the recitation of the Qur'an, so he said to 'Uthman, "O chief of the Believers! Save this nation before they differ about the Book (Qur'an) as Jews and the Christians did before."
> So 'Uthman sent a message to Hafsa saying, "Send us the manuscripts of the Qur'an so that we may compile the Qur'anic materials in perfect copies and return the manuscripts to you." Hafsa sent it to 'Uthman. 'Uthman then ordered Zaid bin Thabit, 'Abdullah bin AzZubair, Said bin Al-As and 'AbdurRahman bin Harith bin Hisham to rewrite the manuscripts in perfect copies. <u>'Uthman said to the three Quraishi men, "In case you disagree with Zaid bin Thabit on any point in the Qur'an, then write it in the dialect of Quraish, the Qur'an was revealed in their tongue.</u>" They did so, and when they had written many copies, 'Uthman returned the original manuscripts to Hafsa. 'Uthman sent to every Muslim province one copy of what they had copied, and ordered that all the other Qur'anic materials, whether written in fragmentary manuscripts or whole copies, be burnt. Said bin Thabit added, "A Verse from Surat Ahzab was

missed by me when we copied the Qur'an and I used to hear Allah's Apostle reciting it. So we searched for it and found it with Khuzaima bin Thabit Al-Ansari. (That Verse was): 'Among the Believers are men who have been true in their covenant with Allah.' (33.23)" (*Sahih Bukhari*, Vol.6, Book 61, Hadith Number 510)

Although the Qur'an was compiled into one book during Abu Bakr's rule, by the time Uthman ibn Affan the third Caliph (644-656 A.D.) came to power there appeared many versions and copies of the Qur'an in the hands of Muslims which caused much confusion among the religiously conscientious Muslims. This had prompted Uthman to prepare a newer edition of the copy that was made during Abu Bakr's time. This time Uthman designated few others to work with Zaid in order to 'correct him' in preparing the official version of the Qur'an.

Questions to Muslims

Question#1: Since there was already the first complied version of the Qur'an during Abu Bakr's time, where was the need for Uthman to compile another one?

Question#2: If Abu Bakr's version of the Qur'an was a 'perfect' Qur'an, then why would Uthman expect any disagreements between Zaid and the others in making copies from that Qur'an?

Question#3: If the existing copies were not in conflict with each other, then where is the need for Uthman to produce another official and standard version of the Qur'an instead of just choosing one out of those many copies that were already available and making copies of them without any corrections based on the disagreement of the three Quraishi men?

Question#4: Even if Uthman wanted to produce a beautiful and systematic new official version of the Qur'an based on the Abu Bakr's version and the corrections of three Quraishi men, and send the copies of the official one to the other parts of the then Muslim world where then is the need for him to destroy all those collected Qur'anic copies including the *whole copies* by fire if they were indeed not conflicting with each other in significant ways?

Once the scribes had prepared a standard version of the Qur'an under Uthman's directives based primarily on the Abu Bakr's version but along with the three Quraishi men's corrections wherever they differed with Zaid, Uthman destroyed all the previous copies that had been made and collected. In the Hadiths we are told that from the Uthman's Standard Version of the Qur'an four more copies were made and sent to four different Islamic centers in the world at that time.

Some Muslims claim unsuccessfully that those copies are still available today. The fact is none of them exists. No substantial proof has been offered to the contrary till today. One Muslim scholar while discussing one of the oldest Qur'anic manuscripts the Samarkand Manuscript candidly admitted, "So, the big question now is whether this is the Qur'an that belonged to the third caliph 'Uthmān? The answer is no. There are good number of other Qur'ans [such as the one at St. Petersburg, two in Istanbul (Topkapi Library and TIEM), and two in Cairo (al-Hussein mosque and Dār al-Kutub)] having at times turned up in different parts of the Islamic world, <u>some purporting to show traces of blood from the third caliph 'Uthmān upon certain pages</u>, and thus the genuine 'Uthmānic Qur'an, the IMĀM, which he was reading at the time of his death." [S.al-Munajjid, *Dirāsāt fī Tārīkh al-Khatt al-'Arabī Mundhu Bidayatihi ilā Nihayat al-'Asr al-Umawi*, 1972, Dar al-Kitab al-Jadid: Beirut (Lebanon), pp. 50-51]

In order to convince the world that the mysterious Uthmanic Version of the Qur'an still exists, faithful Muslims have gone to the extent of painting the 'blood stains' of Uthman on several manuscripts which are otherwise known as fake ones. Of course, undoubtedly these adventures were undertaken by faithful Muslim devotees in order to provide the much needed support to their religious convictions with noble intentions. Such is the fervor of the followers of Islam in garnering the support for the authenticity of the Quran!

Question to Muslims

Question#1: Which of the two Qur'ans—Abu Bakr's version and Uthman's version—is the original Qur'an?

Question#2: Why do these two Qur'ans not exist today?

Although the Abu Bakr version of the Qur'an had been returned to Hafsa soon after the official Uthmanic version of the Qur'an was prepared, apparently it was also destroyed later in fire by Marwan bin Hakam, Uthman's secretary, in 684 A.D. in line with Uthman's order to burn all the Qur'anic materials other than the official ones.

Apart from the above, Uthman is also credited with the destruction of six *ahrufs* out of seven that were supposedly given by the Islamic prophet Muhammad. It needs to be stated here that the Quran was reportedly revealed in **seven different *ahrufs*** or ways or modes (versions) as the following tradition records:

Narrated 'Umar bin Al-Khattab:

I heard Hisham bin Hakim reciting Surat-al-Furqan during the lifetime of Allah's Apostle, I listened to his recitation and noticed that he was reciting in a way that Allah's Apostle had not taught me. I was about to jump over him while he was still in prayer, but I waited patiently and when he finished his prayer, I put my sheet round his neck (and pulled him) and said, "Who has taught you this Sura which I have heard you reciting?" Hisham said, "Allah's Apostle taught it to me." I said, "You are telling a lie, for he taught it to me in a way different from the way you have recited it!" Then I started leading (dragged) him to Allah's Apostle and said (to the Prophet), "I have heard this man reciting Surat-al-Furqan in a way that you have not taught me." The Prophet said: "(O 'Umar) release him! Recite, O Hisham." Hisham recited in the way I heard him reciting. Allah's Apostle said, "It was revealed like this."
"Then Allah's Apostle said, "Recite, O 'Umar!" I recited in the way he had taught me, whereupon he said, "It was revealed like this," and added, "The Qur'an has been revealed to be recited in seven different ways, so recite of it whichever is easy for you." (*Sahih al-Bukhari*, Volume 9, Book 93, Number 640)

Questions to Muslims

Question#1: If Allah had given his Qur'an in seven different modes or ahrufs why did Muslims destroy the majority of them i.e. six ahrufs, while keeping only one?

The Holy Bible: Muslim Objections and Christian Responses

> **Question#2:** In the light of the fact that six ahurfs of the Qur'an were lost forever because Uthman destroyed them intentionally, what guarantee is there that that he had preserved just one ahruf of the Qur'an perfectly well without any changes to his liking?

As a matter of fact, even during Muhammad's time the Qur'an, which is supposedly preserved in Heaven, had to be re-written and re-phrased to facilitate a better construction of the sentences as the following *Hadith* testifies:

> "It has been narrated on the authority of Abu Ishaq, that he heard Bara' talking about the Qur'anic verse: "Those who sit (at home) from among the believers and those who go out for Jihad in the way of Allah are not equal" (Qur'an S. 4:95). (He said that) the Messenger of Allah (may peace be upon him) ordered Zaid (to write the verse). He brought a shoulder-blade (of a slaughtered camel) and inscribed it (the verse) thereon. The son of Umm Maktum complained of his blindness to the Holy Prophet (may peace be upon him). (At this) descended the revelation: "Those of the believers who sit (at home) <u>without any trouble</u> (illness, incapacity, disability)" (Qur'an S. 4:95). The tradition has been handed down through two other chains of transmitters." (*Sahih Muslim*, Book 20, Hadith Number 4676)

According to the above *Hadith* the Qur'anic verse 4:95 was initially revealed as *'Those who sit (at home) from among the believers and...'*

However, when a blind Muslim heard this he complained about his disability to the Islamic prophet Muhammad and because of that Muhammad gave another improved version of the verse, apparently by correcting or editing the first one, as *'Those of the believers who sit (at home) without any trouble (without any disability) from among the believers and...'* At least in this verse of the Qur'an i.e. 4:95, the Qur'an was rephrased because of the complaints of a blind man!

In spite of the above facts Muslims claim that the Qur'an is perfectly preserved without even an iota of change or lost and therefore it is from Allah! Objective thinkers and truth seekers see no substance in this claim of Muslims.

> **Questions to Muslims**
>
> **Question#1:** Dear Muslims, if you think that the Qur'an in Arabic is preserved perfectly from the time of your prophet Muhammad till today, please tell us what is the exact number of the total words used in the Arabic Qur'an? Is it 77,277 or 77,430 or 77,437 or 77,439 or 77,934?
>
> **Question#2:** If the Qur'an (Arabic) is perfectly preserved all these centuries then there must be only one Qur'an in the whole world. If there is only one Qur'an in the whole world, why do different Muslim scholars have come up with different numbers for the total Arabic words contained in the Qur'an?

Islamic sources provide enough evidence to contradict the Muslims' claim. That is why Abdullah ibn Umar had said in the very early days of Islam,

> "Let none of you say 'I have acquired the whole of the Qur'an'. How does he know what all of it is when much of the Qur'an has disappeared? Rather let him say 'I have acquired what has survived.'" (As-Suyuti, *Al Itqan fii 'Ulum al-Qur'an*, p. 524).

a) The Qur'an itself implies that Muslims did tamper with its text.

> Qur'an: Surat Al-Hijr (The Rocky Tract) 15:90-93
>
> كَمَا أَنزَلْنَا عَلَى الْمُقْتَسِمِينَ الَّذِينَ جَعَلُوا الْقُرْآنَ عِضِينَ فَوَرَبِّكَ لَنَسْأَلَنَّهُمْ أَجْمَعِينَ عَمَّا كَانُوا يَعْمَلُونَ
>
> "(Of just such wrath) as We sent down on those who divided (Scripture into arbitrary parts),-*(So also on such) as <u>have made Qur'an into shreds</u> (as they please). Therefore, by the Lord, We will, of a surety, call them to account, For all their deeds."

b) According to some reliable Muslim traditions called authentic Hadiths whole surahs are missing in the present-day Qur'ans:

> "<u>We used to recite a surah</u> which resembled in length and severity to (Surah) *Bara'at*. I have, however, forgotten it with the exception of this which I remember out of it: "If there were two valleys full of riches, for the son of Adam, he would long for a third valley, and nothing would fill the stomach of the son of Adam but dust". (*Sahih Muslim*, Book 5, Hadith Number 2286)

"And we used so recite a surah which resembled one of the surahs of Musabbihat, and I have forgotten it, but remember (this much) out of it: "Oh people who believe, why do you say that which you do not practise" (lxi 2.) and "that is recorded in your necks as a witness (against you) and you would be asked about it on the Day of Resurrection" (S. 17:13)." (*Sahih Muslim*, Book 5, Hadith Number 2286)

c) According to authentic Hadiths whole verses are missing in today's version of the Qur'an:

"'Abdullah b. 'Abbas reported that 'Umar b. Khattab sat on the pulpit of Allah's Messenger (may peace be upon him) and said: Verily Allah sent Muhammad (may peace be upon him) with truth and He sent down the Book upon him, and the verse of stoning was included in what was sent down to him. We recited it, retained it in our memory and understood it. Allah's Messenger (may peace be upon him) awarded the punishment of stoning to death (to the married adulterer and adulteress) and, after him, we also awarded the punishment of stoning, I am afraid that with the lapse of time, the people (may forget it) and may say: We do not find the punishment of stoning in the Book of Allah, and thus go astray by abandoning this duty prescribed by Allah. Stoning is a duty laid down in Allah's Book for married men and women who commit adultery when proof is established, or if there is pregnancy, or a confession." (Chapter 4: Stoning of a married adulterer, *Sahih Muslim*, Book 17, Hadith Number 4194 & *Sahih Al-Bukhari*, Book 8, Hadith Number 817)

"Narrated by Ibn 'Abbas...And then we used to recite among the Verses in Allah's Book: 'O people! Do not claim to be the offspring of other than your fathers, as it is disbelief (unthankfulness) on your part that you claim to be the offspring of other than your real father'..." (*Sahih Al-Bukhari*, Volume 8, Book 82, Hadith Number 817)

"Narrated by Anas bin Malik...For thirty days Allah's Apostle invoked Allah to curse those who had killed the companions of Bir-Mauna; he invoked evil upon the tribes of Ral, Dhakwan, and Usaiya who disobeyed Allah and His Apostle. There was reveled about those who were killed at Bir-Mauna a Qur'anic Verse we used to recite, but it was cancelled later on. The Verse was: "Inform our people that we have met our Lord. He is pleased with us and He has made us pleased" (*Sahih Al-Bukhar*, Volume 4, Hadith Number 69)

"'A'isha (Allah be pleased with, her) reported that it had been revealed in the Holy Qur'an that ten clear sucklings make the marriage unlawful, then it was abrogated (and substituted) by five sucklings and Allah's Apostle (may peace be upon him) died and it was before that time (found) in the Holy Qur'an (and recited by the Muslims)." (*Sahih Muslim*, Book 8, Hadith Number 3421)

d) The ancient copies of the Qur'an prove that there are many variant readings in the text of the Qur'an.

There are only a handful of ancient Qur'anic MSS available today from before eighth century as opposed to the thousands of ancient Biblical MSS available today from the same period of time.

The following six ancient Qur'anic MSS are the most significant ones that come from between late seventh century and early ninth century:

i) *Sana Manuscripts* (670-715 A.D.) Sana, Yemen. It has only half of the Qur'anic text. It differs frequently from the standard Qur'anic text. It has over a thousand variants in comparison to the modern-day popular Qur'an.

ii) *Codex Parisino-Petropolitanus* (690-720 A.D.) in Paris, Frans. It contains 40% Qur'anic text. It has many differences with the standard Qur'anic text. Most of the differences are orthographic in nature but a significant number of them are considered to be copyist's mistakes.

iii) *Cairo Mushaf* (720-25 A.D.) in Egypt National Library, Cairo, Egypt.

iv) *Topkapi Manuscript* (710-750 A.D.) in Istanbul, Turkey. It has the entire Qur'anic text except 23 verses. According to a Muslim scholar (Tayyar Altikulash) there are 2270 variants readings between this manuscript and the modern-day popular Qur'an.

v) *Samarkand Manuscript* (780-810 A.D.) in Tashkent. It has only one third of the Qur'an text.

vi) *Ma'il Script Manuscript* (790 A.D.) London, UK. It has surahs up to 43.

The modern versions of the Qur'an are based on the Qur'anic text that was standardized by the Islamic scholars in 1924. There is no single Qur'anic manuscript dated before 1924 that perfectly matches to the current versions of the Qur'an.

Every single ancient copy of the Qur'an has multiple variant readings - most are unimportant but some are viable - in comparison to the modern versions of the Qur'an that are in use in the world today. Christian apologist Samuel Green noted,

'There are approximately **100 textual differences** between the ancient Samarkand manuscript and the modern edition of the Qur'an.' The evidence of this fact has been presented with a comparison between the Samarkand manuscript text and the modern day text at:
http://answering-islam.org/PQ/A1.htm#AppendA.

e) The modern day Qur'ans also differ from each other in their Arabic letters, words, and meanings. Muslims claim that the text of the Qurans used by Muslims all over the world is identical letter for letter. This is a false claim based on religious fanaticism. Different Qur'anic versions are in use in different parts of the world even today. For example, 'Warsh version' of the Qur'an is in use in the North African countries such as Algeria, Morocco, Parts of Tunisia, West Africa and Sudan; 'Qalun version' of the Qur'an is in use in countries such as Libya, Tunisia and parts of Qatar; 'al-Duri version' of the Qur'an is in use in places such as parts of Sudan and West Africa; 'Hafs version' of the Qur'an is in use in the Muslim world in general.

Do all these versions of the Qur'an perfectly match with each other? No! If we compare two versions of the Qur'an, the Hafs version and the Warsh version, there are nearly 1354 small differences between these two current versions of the Qur'an alone. Let's see five examples of the variant readings between these two versions of the Qur'an—Hafs and Warsh:

The comparison table is on the next page.

Variant reading	The Hafs version of the Qur'an	The Warsh version of the Qur'an
(1) Extra 'and' in Hafs version!	وَسَارِعُوٓاْ *wasaari'uu* And hasten (wasaari'uu) to ... S. 3:133	سَارِعُوٓاْ *saari'uu* Hasten saari'uu) to ... (S. 3:133
(2) Meaning changes from active to passive!	قَٰتَلَ *qatala* And many a prophet fought (qatala) ... S. 3.146	قُتِلَ *qutila* And many a prophet was killed (qutila)... S. 3.146. (As in S. 3:144 in both versions.)
(3) Meaning changes from referring to the magicians to what the magicians did!	سِحْرَانِ *sihraani* two works of magic ... S. 28:48	سَٰحِرَانِ *saahiraani* two magicians ...S. 28:48
(4) *qaala* is the perfect tense and therefore Muhammad is the subject of the verb, but *qul* is the imperative and therefore the subject is God who is commanding Muhammad/Muslims.	قَالَ *qaala* He said (qaala), "My Lord knows..." S. 21:4	قُلْ *qul* Say (qul): My Lord knows...S. 21:4
(5) There are different letters at the beginning of these words. This difference changes the meaning from "we" to "he"	يُؤْتِيهِم *yu'tiihim* ... he gives them ... (S. 4:152)	نُوتِيهِمُو *nuutiihimuu* ... we give them ... S. 4:151(152)

f) Even if we accept - against all the evidence - that the Qur'an is preserved perfectly, that itself doesn't prove it is from God. If the Harry Potter book is preserved without any change for the next millennia or two still it remains as a fantasy novel, but doesn't become a divinely inspired book owing to its purity in preservation.

Qur'an depends on *Hadiths* (traditions that were circulating among Muslims about Muhammad) for its context, chronology, clarity and validity. But the majority of the Hadiths themselves are unreliable, contradictory and spurious which were collected and codified 150 years after Muhammad's death.

In the light of the above facts it becomes apparent that the Qur'an was given by Muhammad himself on his personal convictions as well as for his personal reasons.

Questions to Muslims

Question#1: According to the science of textual criticism the presence of a number of variant readings in a text does not invalidate the text to be the word of God. Obviously Muslims claim that the Qur'an with its number of variant readings in the ancient manuscripts can pass the test of the textual criticism. We Christians don't have problem with this. However, we ask, by the same standard why can't the Holy Bible with its number of variant readings in the ancient manuscripts pass the test of the textual criticism?

Question#2: If you claim that the Qur'an is perfectly preserved till today, can you show us any two ancient hand-written whole Qur'an manuscripts out of several that survived to this day matching perfectly with each other without a single variant?

Muslim Scholars on the Qur'an

Muslim apologists take special pleasure in appealing to the liberal scholars of the Bible in order to discredit the Bible while showing no tolerance to the view of the liberal scholars of the Qur'an. Here, let's see how two Muslim scholars had viewed the Qur'an from their scholarly study of it. Both of them paid with their lives - like many others in the past - for their honest views of the Quran!

(a) *Ali Dashti*

Ali Dashti is an Iranian Muslim scholar who studied the Qur'an, Hadiths and Islam. He commented on the Qur'an, "The Qur'an contains sentences which are incomplete and not fully intelligible without the aid of commentaries; foreign words, unfamiliar Arabic words, and words used with other than the normal meaning; adjectives and verbs inflected without observance of the concords of gender and number; illogically and ungrammatically applied pronouns which sometimes have no referent; and predicates which in rhymed passages are often remote from the subjects...To sum up, more than one hundred Qur'anic aberrations from the normal rules and structure of Arabic have been noted. Needless to say, the commentators strove to find explanations and justifications of these irregularities.

Among them was the great commentator and philologist Mahmud oz-Zamakhshari (467/1075-538/1144), of whom a Moorish author wrote:
"This grammar-obsessed pedant has committed a shocking error. Our task is not to make the readings conform to Arabic grammar, but to take the whole of the Qur'an as it is and make Arabic grammar conform to the Qur'an."'" (Ali Dashti, *Twenty Three Years: A Study of the Prophetic Career of Muhammad*)

Ali Dashi was honest enough to acknowledge that the Quran has many grammatical errors and aberrations. Therefore it is far from being the perfect literary piece let alone the word of God!

(b) *Dr.Rashad Kalifa*

Dr. Rashad Kalifa is the Muslim scholar who is credited with the discovery of the so-called 'mathematical miracle of the Qur'an,' which has already been proved to be the result of a mere wishful thinking, that many Muslims are fond of quoting even these days. Kalifa's admirers has this to say about his 'notable' find about the Qur'an, "The Mathematical Miracle of the Qur'an proved beyond doubt that every sura, verse, word, and letter in the Qur'an have been under the control and the protection of the Author of the Qur'an. This miracle proved itself as it singled out, the ONLY two verses that have been always suspicious to be an addition to the Qur'an, that is verses 9:128, 129. These two verses have been historically known to be the ONLY questionable verses in the collection of the Qur'an after the death of the prophet Muhammed. It was not Dr. Khalifa who made these verses suspicious, nor was he aware that the Mathematical Miracle of the Qur'an will single them out. The Muslim scholars knew for over 1400 years that these two verses were suspicious and listed them as such in the Islamic history books. Many Muslims have never been aware that these two verses were suspicious and were surprised to know they are for the first time. They are even more surprised to know that the mathematical miracle proved these two verses to be a human addition. This discovery proved that God kept his promise from the minute the Qur'an was collected, but the human being was the one who wronged his soul." **(http://submission.org/Khalifa_Issues_Truth.html)**

According to Rashad Kalifa two of the verses (Sura 9:128-129) in the current Quran are, in fact, later additions.

Muslims' rejection of the Bible as God's word makes perfect sense when we realize in order for a person to accept Muhammad as a prophet like the prophets of the Bible, the Qur'an he gave is also from the same God who gave the Bible, and the Qur'anic Allah he proclaimed is the same God of the Bible one must detach oneself completely from the truth of the Bible, albeit at the cost of his or her own eternal life. In fact, it is this reality that forced many a Muslim to attack the Bible in their effort to earn the ever elusive legitimacy and authenticity for Islam. The Bible and the Quran are mutually exclusive. One must choose either the Bible or the Quran, but not both of them.

If the Christian Scripture (N.T.) is compared with the Muslim Scripture (Qur'an) the contrast is obvious to the objective observer. In search of the true word of God one must ask oneself: Which of these two books is being used in forming the ideologies that justify the oppression of the outsiders, create unrest, promote violence and glorify suicide bombings? Which of these two books exemplifies and promotes love, forgiveness, peace and goodwill even towards enemies?

The Holy Bible: Muslim Objections and Christian Responses

THE SUMMARY OF THE MUSLIM BELIEFS AND CHRISTIAN POSITION ON THEM

Muslim belief	Christian position	Reason for Christian position
(1) The true God whose name is Allah has sent the Qur'an as his word.	This cannot be true!	a. The name of the true God is YHWH or YaHWeH as He Himself revealed it to the true prophet Moses (Ex.3:14-15). b. The God YaHWeH has already warned not to believe if any so-called prophet comes in the name of another god.
(2) It is the angel Gabriel who brought the Qur'an from Allah.	This is highly questionable in the light of God's word the Bible!	a. The Bible warns us that even Satan can disguise himself as an angel of light. (2Cor.11:14) b. Never before the angel Gabriel behaved with the people he was communicating the way it was described in the case of Muhammad.
(3) Prophet Muhammad recited before his followers only what he had received from Gabriel.	This is unfounded claim at best.	a. Quite a number of recitations have to do with promoting Muhammad's personal agendas. b. Many instructions given through these revelations were later changed. c. Most of the revelations are in direct conflict with the Jewish Scriptures (Old Testament) and Christian Scriptures (New Testament).
(4) Prophet Muhammad's first followers faithfully preserved and	This is contrary to the evidence present even in the Islamic sources.	a. But according to Hadiths some chapters (surahs) are missing! b. According to Hadiths some verses are also

passed on the Qur'an.		missing!
(5) Under the first Caliph Umar Zaid compiled the Qur'an perfectly.	It is a statement that cannot be verified.	a. If that were true, then there would not have been many competing and conflicting individual copies evolving after that compilation. b. Even if it were perfectly compiled, it doesn't prove that it was from God!
(6) Under the third Caliph Uthman Zaid compiled the Qur'an again perfectly.	Hardly an acceptable statement!	a. If Zaid had already compiled a 'perfect' Qur'an during Abu Bakr's rule there would not have been the need for collecting various differing copies of the Qur'an and based on them prepare another 'perfect' Qur'an! b. Neither the first so-called 'perfect' Qur'an nor the second so-called 'perfect' Qur'an exists today.
(7) Today's Qur'an is exactly the same as the first Qur'an that was recited by prophet Muhammad.	Far from the truth!	a. Islamic sources provide enough evidence to the contrary to the Muslims' claim. b. Comparison of the modern-day Qur'an with the ancient copies reveals many variant readings. c. Even among the modern-day Qur'ans there are variant readings. d. The fact that Muslims destroyed six ahrufs gives reasons to doubt their trustworthiness in preserving the seventh one without any change!

From the perspective of non-Muslims it is reasonable to say that the Qur'an...

- *Is not complete, which is why Muslims need the Sunna to guide them.*
- *Is not clear, which is why Muslims need Tafsirs or commentaries to clarify.*
- *Is not consistent, which is why Muslims need the 'law of abrogation' to explain away the conflicting statements in it.*
- *Is not fully Arabic, for it has many words of non-Arabic origin such as 'Adam,' 'Dawud,' 'Injeel,' 'Towrah' etc.*
- *Is not perfect, for it is incomplete, unclear, inconsistent and has many errors too.*
- *Is not perfectly preserved, for much of it was lost in the battle of Yamamah in December 632 A.D.*

5. MUSLIM QUESTIONS AND CHRISTIAN ANSWERS

While dealing with religious texts one must be aware of the fact that the Scriptures of any religion can be interpreted in more than one way. Unfortunately, more often than not the Muslims who seek to discredit the Bible try to find faults with it by their inconsistent approaches to the Bible and the Qur'an. They use one standard for the Bible to disprove its authenticity and another standard for the Qur'an to prove its authenticity. This is a blatant hypocrisy. By using such double standard the Muslim thinks he or she can 'prove' that there are substantial problems with the Bible.

For example, if I argue and say, 'The Bible is God's word, but look at the Qur'an, it was not written in English or Hindi. Since the Qur'an was written in Arabic which is a foreign language it's not from God!' Apart from many logical problems we can see in my statement here, my argument is plainly wrong because it is based on double standard. While the Bible itself was not written in English or Hindi how can I object to the fact that the Qur'an was not written in English or Hindi? While the Bible was written in Hebrew, Aramaic and Greek, which are foreign languages, how can I find fault with the Qur'an that was written in Arabic? That's the way hypocrites argue.

Typical Muslim questions or arguments against the Bible are based on their misunderstanding or misreading of the text and context. While there are tons of problems with the Qur'an and its contents they overlook all that and tend to find fault with the Bible in an effort to undermine its authenticity. Some of the questions and objections they have might be genuine and worth addressing, but most of them are trifling and lack substance.

The Holy Bible: Muslim Objections and Christian Responses

Recently on a Facebook group discussion two Muslim women began to bombard me with rather childish questions. One of them claimed that she was a Christian before she had found out that the Bible has contradictions. I asked for an example of such contradictions. She told me that the Bible has two different and conflicting statements about who created the world: in one place the Bible says God created the world and in another place Jesus created it. She asked how this can be.

In response, I told her it is God who created all that exists through His inner Word and that same inner Word of God took on human form and nature and became Jesus Christ. Then I asked her where the contradiction she had seen was in that particular issue. Ignoring both my answer and my question completely she came up with another such question. Such people are obviously not really seeking the truth.

Several years ago I met and befriended Tahir a Muslim young man. During our spiritual discussions he would argue blindly that the Bible is wrong. One day I asked him why he thought so. I put this in a casual and non-confronting question form before him. His answer was revealing as well as distressing. He told me that his Mullah (Islamic religious leader) had told him that the Bible is wrong and therefore he should not read it. This has convinced Tahir not only to keep himself away from the Bible but also spread the 'news of this danger' to others.

It is a pity that the world is full of prideful people who reject the truth simply because it doesn't make sense to them or fit into their limited understanding. Or it could be that they simply hate light and truth that were given to them, as the Bible predicts they would. Some reject the very existence of the Creator, some reject certain actions of the Creator, some reject the demonstration of the love of the Creator towards them and some reject the great salvation that the Creator offers them on His own terms!

Over the years, I have met countless number of Muslims who are quick to talk evil about the Bible even though they had never read it themselves. Some of them would freak out if the Bible is given to them. They are extremely hesitant even to touch it and open it and read its contents in order to find the truth about it for themselves.

One of the ways Muslims are being kept hostage by Islam is through the indoctrination of false information about the Bible. Muslims are warned by their Islamic religious leaders not to read the Bible, lest it should do something bad to them. Yes, the Bible surely does something to Muslims if they open its pages and read its contents, but definitely not something that is undesirable for them. Rather, what it does is to offer them what they (and we!) don't deserve at all, namely forgiveness and eternal life from God! This is becoming a common story in the Muslim countries in the East.

Let me tell you about Shaukrat and Omar - two sincere Muslims, neighbours as well as relatives who grew up with the same Bible-suspecting mentality. This attitude towards the Bible kept them 'safe' from the truth of the Bible until the year 2000. But one fateful day that year without realizing they stumbled upon the message of the 'Injeel' (New Testament) described in a small pamphlet given to them in their native language by an old Christian lady. Both were struck by the power and the truth of those words in that pamphlet. This encounter ultimately led them to find forgiveness and eternal life as offered freely in the 'Injeel' (N.T.).

Their journey in this new-found faith was far from being a joy-ride all along. Their family members and the whole Muslim community turned against them. At one point they were about to be stoned to death. They did not shrink back. God intervened and spared their lives. Both of them are now busy spreading the blessed news they have found in the 'Injeel' to other Muslims. By now most of their family members have embraced Christ. In the past ten years of my association with them, I've been humbled by their unwavering faith and have learnt a lot from their passion for evangelism.

In contrast, many so-called Christians in the West in recent days are being fooled into believing that the Bible has contradictions or errors and therefore the only alternatives now left are the Quran and Islam. Thus many have left their former religious association with some form of Christianity, and have embraced Islam.

Does this in anyway undermine the authenticity of the Bible as God's word? Absolutely not! Instead, this phenomenon only serves as a confirmation of the fact that the Bible is God's word, for it demonstrates the fulfillment of the prophecy given in the Bible two thousand years ago:

"The Spirit clearly says that in later times some will abandon the faith and follow deceiving spirits and things taught by demons. Such teachings come through hypocritical liars, whose consciences have been seared as with a hot iron." (1Tim.4:1-2)

Who could have given two thousand years ago such a striking prediction of the reality of these days, if it were not for divine inspiration? With this in mind, let's examine the most common and significant objections Muslims level against the Bible and see if they hold any water, particularly when we apply the same criteria in examining the Muslims' holy book the Qur'an.

LIES OF THE EVIL ONE

Beware of the lies of the evil one! Before we investigate the alleged problems with the Bible first we must be mindful of the following lies perpetuated by the deceiver Satan who is the enemy of the truth of God:

- God doesn't exist! Creation created itself!
- Even if God exists, He didn't or doesn't speak to people!
- Even if God spoke, His words are not recorded for mankind!
- Even if God's words are recorded, His words are not acceptable for they are not to the liking of some people!
- Even if God's words are acceptable to some people, His words are corrupted implying that God failed to protect them!
- Even if God's words are not corrupted and are protected by God, His words have become obsolete now for new words have come in their place!

It is vitally important to ask the Muslim who questions the authenticity of the Bible based on his or her fallacious assumptions the following relevant questions and see if his or her responses are consistent with his or her beliefs about the Qur'an as well:

1. What can and cannot be included in Allah's (God's) word and why?
2. Does Allah (God) have the freedom and the right to recount in His word past events - both evil and good - or not?
3. Can Allah (God) preserve His word even in the midst of some copies with variant readings in them or not?

In this section we will examine nearly 75 common accusations, objections and questions raised by Muslims against the Bible, and also see the appropriate responses to them. Every single problem both critiques and Muslims 'see' in the Bible is rooted in one of the following factors:

a. *Misunderstanding or misreading the context*: Failing to take the immediate as well as larger contexts of the verses into consideration can cause the reader to misunderstand the Bible. Sometimes commentaries and other biblical aids can help overcome this problem.
b. *Missing or mistaking the intended meanings of the words in their original languages*: Sometimes translations can obscure or confuse the meaning of the verses in the Bible. Therefore, in such cases it is critical to consult the original language aids to get to the proper meaning of the Bible. Hebrew, Aramaic and Greek lexicons could provide valuable help in this case. Consulting different translations can also help get out of the confusion caused by this factor.
c. *Failing to recognize literary expressions*: Like any other literature, sacred or secular, the Bible employs numerous literary styles and devices. Therefore it is important to understand the message of the Bible through the particular literary expression it employed in a particular place. For example, wherever the text contains

metaphorical or figurative expression there one should not understand the text in literal sense, and vice versa. Here too commentaries can be of great help. Instead of consulting only one commentary it is always safer that one should consult as many commentaries as possible in order to ascertain the appropriate meaning of the text of the Bible.

d. *The presence of mistakes or errors caused by copyists in some manuscript copies*: Thousands of ancient manuscript copies of the Bible are available today. All hand-written manuscripts – Christian, Muslim or secular – were prone to copyist mistakes. This, however, doesn't affect the original message. The apparent conflicts arise due to this factor can easily be cleared by consulting different ancient manuscripts that are available or the translations of the Bible that used them.

It goes without saying that no one translation of the Bible in any language from their original languages – Hebrew, Aramaic and Greek - is perfect. Therefore, when we come across a seemingly contradictory or confusing account in the Scriptures before jumping to conclude that the Scriptures are erroneous it is necessary to consider their contexts and consult those Scriptures in different translations as well as in their original languages to ascertain the truth.

Accusation # 1: *The Bible is a compilation of mere human accounts but not God's word!*

Response: Totally wrong! This is purely an unfounded opinion of the unbelievers. The very unity among the sixty-six books, given that they are from different times, places, languages and individuals itself bears witness to the fact that it is but from one supernatural author and thus confirms its divine origin. In addition, within the theistic world view God exists and He spoke to human beings. Those words of God have been preserved in recorded form for future generations. That's what the Bible is.

It's true that the Bible was not thrown out from heaven to earth! As a matter of fact no book ever came that way. The Bible was not written by God nor dictated verbatim by Him. Rather it was written by men chosen by God, but authored by God through His divine inspiration or superintendence. That's what makes the Bible God's word.

As far as the authenticity of the Bible is concerned it is confirmed beyond a shadow of doubt, as discussed in the previous chapters. If Muslims do not want to consider the Bible as God's word or Allah's word, then they have to show us where the 'Previous Scriptures' (Tawraat, Zaboor, Injeel, writings and prophets cf. Quran: Sura 2:136 & 3:48) are that the Quran came to confirm and often refers to. This is all too important as the Quran itself advises Christians and Jews to follow and be judged by their scriptures. If those 'Previous Scriptures' do not exist anymore, how can the Quran, which is supposedly the eternal word of Allah, instruct Jews and Christians to follow those scriptures? Does that mean the Quran is not the eternal word of Allah for all mankind for all times, but only meant for the people in Arabia during the Islamic prophet Muhammad's time?

Apart from the above problems, the fact is that hundreds of ancient copies of the Bible that we have today date from the second to sixth century which predate the beginning of Islam or the life of its prophet in the early seventh century. This raises another problem for Muslims: From the Quran's instructions we understand at least during the Islamic prophet Muhammad's time the 'Previous Scriptures' (Tawraat and Injeel) did exist and the Jews and Christians of his time had them in their hands. Those same scriptures are what we have today in the form of the Bible. However, if Muslims think otherwise, they should explain to us what happened to those 'Previous Scriptures' after their prophet's time.

Accusation # 2: *The Bible i.e. The Tawraat, Zaboor and Injeel, was originally Allah's word (God's word), but later it has been corrupted and changed by Jews and Christians.*

Response: This is completely false! The sworn enemy of God and God's truth is the devil i.e. Satan. It is Satan who engineered countless lies against God and God's truth. The saying, 'God's word has been corrupted or changed' is one of Satan's biggest lies against God and His truth. It is sad and unfortunate that many people unwittingly fall prey to this trap of the devil. The Bible (Tawraat, Zaboor, the Prophets and the Injeel), as given in original autographs, has been given by God to mankind and the full message of those autographs has been kept intact by God Himself.

(a) Theological response
God exists. He spoke to mankind through His chosen ones. He also made sure that His words are recorded for future generations. The same God ensured the safe transmission and protection of His words as He Himself assured them (Is. 40:8; Mat.5:18; Lk.21:33; Heb.2:2; 1Pet.1:25).

(b) Biblical response
God's word cannot be corrupted since God is able to keep His word (message) safe and intact from any corruption. He who does not believe this undeniable truth is an unbeliever of the worst kind. God's promises make sure that His word remains unalterable forever (Is.40:8; Mat.5:18; Heb.2:2; 1Pet.1:24-25). The manuscript copies or translations of the original autographs of the Scripture are only the vehicles that carry the original message i.e. God's word, across generations till the end. However, it is quite possible for intentional or unintentional changes or mistakes to creep into *some* of the copies of the original word of God. This doesn't mean by any stretch of imagination that the original word of God has also been corrupted! Copies and translations are a later development. Changes or mistakes in some of the copies or translations cannot affect the original autographs of the Bible whose contents are being protected and also transmitted from generation to generation under God's supervision.

In the light of the above assertions the original word of God has been passed down to us in the form of at least one of the thousands of the copies that we now have. God's word (The Bible) abides forever!

If one argues against this truth, one needs to produce the

original autographs of the Bible that are different from the current Bible since the burden of proof rests solely on the unbeliever or the skeptic. Without such evidence all talk about corruption of the Bible is a baseless as well as a serious accusation against God Himself.

(c) Rational response

By the middle of the sixth century, the scriptures of Jews and Christians – with hundreds of hand written copies - were spread across not only the little Hijaz, but all over Asia Minor, North Africa and Southern Europe.

It would be literally impossible to collect all those copies and convince all the warring sects within Judaism and Christianity to agree to make similar changes or corruptions on all of them. Even if such a miraculous collusion had taken place without any publicity, what could be the reason behind it? Why in the world would all these differing people agree to take such an unthinkable and blasphemous action? What were they hoping to gain? Honest answers to these questions reveal to us that the accusation of the corruption in the Bible is an big lie without any valid substance.

Question to Muslims

Question: According to the Qur'an Tawraat, Zaboor, Injeel and Qur'an are Allah's words (S. 5:43-47; 21:105). According to the Qur'an no one can change Allah's words or Allah's words cannot be changed (S. 6:34, 115). But you Muslims say that Allah's words Tawraat, Zaboor and Injeel have been changed and corrupted. Now we Christians ask, are you telling the truth or the Qur'an is telling the truth? Please remember, if you are telling the truth, then the Qur'an is false. Or else, what the Qur'an says is true, then what you are telling is a lie.

Objection # 3: *The New Testament is not written by prophets and therefore it is not from God.*
Response: This demonstrates the ignorance of the interlocutor. Nowhere has God made it a rule that the Scripture or God's word must be given only through prophets. In fact, the O.T. Scriptures

The Holy Bible: Muslim Objections and Christian Responses

were given through and recorded by not only prophets but also priests, kings, governors, singers etc. God in His sovereignty gives His word through divine inspiration. God gives this divine inspiration to the people of His choice. It could be any of God's servants. During Jesus' time the inspiration for the recording of the Scriptures were given to some of the apostles and evangelists purely based on God's freedom of choice.

Question to Muslims

Question: If you say the NT (Injeel) is not from God because it was not written by the prophets, then do you agree by the same standard that the Qur'an is also not from God because it was not written by any Prophet or even the Islamic prophet Muhammad himself?

Objection # 4: *We don't even know the names of the authors of some of the books of the Bible. Therefore it is not Allah's (God's) word.*

Response: Let's deal with this objection. The books of the Bible were written by men chosen by God. This fact is attested by the witness, acceptance and treatment of these books by their contemporaries as well as the testimonies of the chosen men of God in subsequent eras. In reality, all the names of the inspired writers of the books of the Bible are known except a couple of them where there seems to be some ambiguity with regard to the certainty of the names. But the bottom line is that all the books of the Bible are given through divinely inspired men of God.

Questions to Muslims

Quesition#1: Out of 66 books of the Holy Bible only eight of them have little ambiguity with regard to the names of their writers. The rest of the names of the writers of the books are confirmed. So, if you have objections to believe in the books whose authors names are not known, then do you believe those books whose authors we do know as God's word?

Question#2: If the fact that the names of the writers of a few books of the Holy Bible are not known is a reason to reject the whole Holy Bible as God's word, then can you tell us who wrote down the first Surah of the Qur'an i.e. Al Fatiha, when it was first recited by the Islamic prophet Muhammad? Or the names of any of the 114 Surahs of the Qur'an?

Question#3: Although some Hadith literature alludes to the names of around forty scribes who were supposedly recorded the Qur'an as it was recited by Muhammad, yet since no one knows which Surah of the Qur'an was written down by which scribe, why can't the whole Qur'an be discarded as not from Allah according to your own logic?

Objection # 5: *Even many Christian scholars say that the Bible is changed and it is not the perfect word of God. Therefore the Bible is not from Allah.*

Response: There are many secular (atheistic) and liberal scholars who do not believe that the Bible is God's word. They have Christian names and some even claim to be Christians, but they are not true Christians. They do not believe in a God who gives His word through inspiration and is also capable of protecting it. They don't believe in miracles, virgin birth etc. According to them not only the Bible but also the Qur'an are mere human accounts or poems!

Question to Muslims

Question: In spite of the fact that many secular scholars who tried to examine the Qur'an from critical point of view were murdered by Muslim religious fanatics, there are some Muslim scholars who were bold enough to say that the Qur'an is not a perfect word of Allah! Based on that do you reject the Qur'an?

Example:

The Iranian-Arab scholar Ali Dashti in his posthumously published book commented on the Qur'an:
Neither the Qur'an's eloquence, nor its moral precepts are miraculous. (Ali Dashti, *Twenty Three Years*, p. 57)

Objection # 6: *Even the Bible has the proof for its corruption in the book of Jeremiah (Jer.8:8). Therefore it is not Allah's (God's) word.*

Response: Let's see what the verse says in its immediate context:
"*How can you say, 'We are wise, and <u>the law of the LORD is with us</u>'? But behold, the lying pen of the scribes has made it into a lie. The wise men are put to shame, they are dismayed and caught; Behold, <u>they have rejected the word</u>*

of the LORD, and what kind of wisdom do they have?" (Jer.8:8-9) NASB

If we read the verse in its proper context it becomes apparent that prophet Jeremiah is rebuking the Jewish scribes of his day for not only writing something and calling it God's word but also rejecting the true word of God i.e. the Torah (Tawraat)! The prophet is not saying anything implying that God's word *viz.* Torah, has been corrupted by the scribes.

Even the enemies of prophet Jeremiah knew that the Law cannot be lost. Here is what they say about the Law:

"Then they said, "Come and let us devise plans against Jeremiah. Surely the law is not going to be lost to the priest, nor counsel to the sage, nor the divine word to the prophet! Come on and let us strike at him with our tongue, and let us give no heed to any of his words." (Jer.18:18) NASB

Question to Muslims

Question: If you think Jer.8:8 is a proof for the corruption of the Torah, then do you also think in the same way when we find similar things in the Qur'an?
Example:
"(Of just such wrath) as We sent down on those who divided (Scripture into arbitrary parts), - (So also on such) as have made Qur'an into shreds (as they please)." (S. 15:90-91)

Objections # 7: *The Bible has several versions. That shows it has undergone modifications by Christians. Therefore it is not Allah's (God's) word.*

Response: The Bible was originally written in three different languages—Hebrew, Aramaic and Greek. Although the original manuscripts are no longer available there are thousands of manuscript copies first made from originals and later from copies available today. These thousands of hand-written available copies are in original languages, beginning from the first century to fifteenth century.

These manuscript copies of the Scriptures have been translated into many languages. In fact, many groups or individuals in different times and places have made separate translations of these copies into English. Any literature when being translated from one language into another can be expressed in several possible ways. One word in a language can have several different meanings in another language. Because of this the Bible has been translated into English many times, by different people in different places. Each translation is termed as a version. All these versions try to bring about the nearest possible meaning to the original language manuscripts. The fact is no single translation can claim 100 percent accuracy in giving the exact meaning of the copies in the original languages.

All these translations or versions of the Bible do not affect or change in any way the original message given in the original languages!

For example, there are many translations of the Qur'an we have today in English alone. Even though Muslim call those translations as the 'meaning of the Qur'an,' do they affect the message of the Qur'an in Arabic language in any way? No! Likewise, the translations or versions of the Bile do not in any way change the meaning of the Bible in its original languages.

> *The Qur'an has several English translations. Muslims prefer to call an English translation of the Qur'an the 'meaning of the Qur'an.' The Bible has several English translations. Christians prefer to call an English translation of the Bible a 'version of the Bible.' If Muslims like to tell Christians "because there are several 'versions of the Bible,' the Bible cannot be God's word," then by the same logic Christians could also say "because there are several 'meanings of the Qur'an,' the Qur'an cannot be God's word, either!*

Objection # 8: *The Bible has same stories/incidents presented with variations. This shows the Bible is unreliable and not Allah's (God's) word.*
Response: The Bible has same stories told differently by different inspired men of God. For example, the gospel narratives were

The Holy Bible: Muslim Objections and Christian Responses

summarized by four different inspired apostles slightly differently. But none of them contradict the others. On the contrary, they complement one another.

Question to Muslims

Question: If the variations in the description of the same incident in different accounts discredit a book to be God's word, then why does the Qur'an describe the same event with several variations in different places? Doesn't this discredit the Qur'an as Allah's word?

Eg. Moses and the burning bush!

(1) "*Has the story of Moses reached thee? Behold, he saw a fire: So he said to his family, "Tarry ye; I perceive a fire; perhaps I can bring you some burning brand therefrom, or find some guidance at the fire." But when he came to the fire, a voice was heard: "O Moses! "Verily I am thy Lord! therefore (in My presence) put off thy shoes: thou art in the sacred valley Tuwa. I have chosen thee: listen, then, to the inspiration (sent to thee). Verily, I am God: There is no god but I: So serve thou Me (only), and establish regular prayer for celebrating My praise. Verily the Hour is coming - My design is to keep it hidden - for every soul to receive its reward by the measure of its Endeavour. Therefore let not such as believe not therein but follow their own lusts, divert thee therefrom, lest thou perish! And what is that in the right hand, O Moses?" He said, "It is my rod: on it I lean; with it I beat down fodder for my flocks; and in it I find other uses." (God) said, "Throw it, O Moses!" He threw it, and behold! It was a snake, active in motion. (God) said, "Seize it, and fear not: We shall return it at once to its former condition. Now draw thy hand close to thy side: It shall come forth white (and shining), without harm (or stain), - as another Sign, -In order that We may show thee (two) of our Greater Signs. Go thou to Pharaoh, for he has indeed transgressed all bounds.*" (S. 20:9-24)

(2) "*Behold! Moses said to his family: "I perceive a fire; soon will I bring you from there some information, or I will bring you a burning brand to light our fuel, that ye may warm yourselves. But when he came to the (fire), a voice was heard: "Blessed are those in the fire and those around: and glory to God, the Lord of the worlds. "O Moses! verily, I am God, the exalted in might, the wise! "Now do thou throw thy rod!" But when he saw it moving (of its own accord) as if it had been a snake, he turned back in retreat, and retraced not his steps: "O Moses!" (it was said), "Fear not: truly, in My presence, those called as apostles have no fear, - "But if any have done wrong and have thereafter substituted good to take the place of evil, truly, I am Oft-Forgiving, Most Merciful. "Now put thy hand into thy bosom, and it will come forth white without stain (or harm): (these are) among the nine Signs (thou wilt take) to Pharaoh and his people: for they are a*

> *people rebellious in transgression." But when Our Signs came to them, that should have opened their eyes, they said: "This is sorcery manifest!" And they rejected those Signs in iniquity and arrogance, though their souls were convinced thereof: so see what was the end of those who acted corruptly!* (S. 27:7-14)
>
> (3) *"Now when Moses had fulfilled the term, and was travelling with his family, he perceived a fire in the direction of Mount Tur. He said to his family: "Tarry ye; I perceive a fire; I hope to bring you from there some information, or a burning firebrand, that ye may warm yourselves." But when he came to the (fire), a voice was heard from the right bank of the valley, from a tree in hallowed ground: "O Moses! Verily I am God, the Lord of the Worlds "Now do thou throw thy rod!" but when he saw it moving (of its own accord) as if it had been a snake, he turned back in retreat, and retraced not his steps: O Moses!" (It was said), "Draw near, and fear not: for thou art of those who are secure. "Move thy hand into thy bosom, and it will come forth white without stain (or harm), and draw thy hand close to thy side (to guard) against fear. Those are the two credentials from thy Lord to Pharaoh and his Chiefs: for truly they are a people rebellious and wicked." He said: "O my Lord! I have slain a man among them, and I fear lest they slay me."* (S. 28:29-33)

Objection # 9: *Some versions of the Bible have a longer ending to Mark's Gospel (16:9-20) and others do not. In the same way, some versions of the Bible contain the story about the woman caught in the act of adultery in John's Gospel (Jn.7:53-8:11). This is a clear evidence to say that the Bible is corrupted and is not from God.*

Response: This objection is shallow and unsound. Despite the fact that these two portions of the NT are missing in most of the ancient manuscript copies for one reason or another, they are present in some ancient manuscripts. The very fact that a handful of the ancient manuscript copies do have both of them corroborates with their contents as well as teachings that dovetail with the rest of the Bible in establishing their authenticity.

Question to Muslims

Question: If you think the fact that some portions of the Holy Bible are missing in some ancient copies makes the Holy Bible unauthentic, then for the same reason are you willing to declare the Qur'an also as unauthentic since one of its ancient codices the Samarkand Codex does not contain many portions of the modern day Qur'an?

The Holy Bible: Muslim Objections and Christian Responses

Objection # 10: *Christians from the major groups such as Catholics, Protestants and Orthodox, have different Bibles with varying number of books in it. Therefore it is not Allah's (God's) word.*

Response: This objection is based on incomplete information. In the following table all the three religious groups and their Scriptures are compared. As far as the 27 Christian Scriptures (N.T.) are concerned all three major groups in Christianity are united. In the same way, as far as the 39 Jewish Scriptures (O.T.) are concerned all three major groups in Christianity have no disagreement. Only the Catholics and the Orthodox groups have added some extra historical writings to the 66 books of the Bible. This in itself does not affect the authenticity of the 66 books of the Bible.

The following table depicts the religious groups and their accepted holy books respectively.

Religious Group	Sacred Book Name (God's Word)	Accepted Previous Scriptures as God's words	Accepted Historical Writings as Inspired/Sacred
Jews	Tanakh— collection of 39 books	-	-
Christians *a. Protestants* *b. Catholics* *c. Orthodox*	New Testament— collection of 27 books Same Same	a. Tanakh/OT(39) b. Tanakh/OT(39) c Tanakh/OT(39)	a. None b. Apocryphal(7) c. Apocryphal(12)
Muslims *a. Sunni* *b. Shia* *c. Sufi*	Qur'an— collections of 114 surahs Same Same	a. ?? None b. ?? None c. ?? None	a. Hadith (6 collectors) b. Hadith (4 collectors) c. Hadith (several)

As we see in the above table, the problem is not so much with the Christians (Protestant) in believing and possessing the true scriptures of God, as with Muslims of the three sects—Sunni, Shia and Sufi. None of them believe, accept and follow, in practice, the Previous Scriptures even though their Quran enjoins them to. Thus Muslims are guilty before Allah with regard to His scriptures as well as His instructions.

Questions to Muslims

Question#1: If some groups of Muslims add some extra suras to the Qur'ans they read does that change or affect the original Qur'an with other Muslims in any way?

Question#2: Muslims are supposed to believe all the books of Allah and should not make any differentiation among them according to the Qur'anic instruction. While Christians believe their Scriptures and do not show any differentiation between their Scriptures (N.T.) and the previous Scriptures (O.T.) by way of putting them together and studying them together, why do Muslims not believe the previous Scriptures as they believe the Qur'an and at the same time make a huge differentiation between the Qur'an and the previous Scriptures by rejecting them?

Accusations of wrong concepts about God

Objection # 11: *The Bible contains embellishments in describing God. That is why it is not from God. For example God in the Bible is asking Cain, 'Where is Abel your brother?' (Gen.4:9) and also had to come down to see the fact that the people in Sodom and Gomorrah were indeed wicked (Gen.18:20-21). These descriptions clearly imply that the God of the Bible lacks omniscience.*

Response: The Bible uses anthropomorphic language in describing God. When we read of God asking a question we should not jump to conclude that He did not know the answer. God in the Bible poses questions in order to force the responder to confess his or her position and commit to the statement he or she makes in the process.

In cases like the one in Genesis chapter 18 where we see God coming down to 'find out' the sins of the people, God looks down or stoops down because He is kind enough to give people another chance and get the confirmation of their sins through personal verification. This doesn't mean that God lacks omniscience. For example, God tested Abraham by asking him to sacrifice his son, Isaac. But when Abraham proved his obedience to God's command, God did not allow Abraham to kill his son. This incident can be seen both in the Bible (Gen.22:1-19) and the Quran (S. 37:99-109). Does that mean God lacked omniscience before Abraham could prove his obedience to God's command? No! It's the way God deals with people in His kindness.

Question to Muslims

Question: If you think that the descriptions of God's testing in the Bible imply that God is not omniscient then don't you think similar verses in the Qur'an imply the same?

Examples:

"If ye have received a blow, the (disbelieving) people have received a blow the like thereof. These are (only) the vicissitudes which We cause to follow one another for mankind, to the end that <u>Allah may know</u> those who believe and may choose witnesses from among you; and Allah loveth not wrong-doers." (S. 3:140)

"And that <u>Allah may prove</u> those who believe, and may blight the disbelievers." (S. 3:141)

"Or deemed ye that ye would enter paradise while yet <u>Allah knoweth not</u> those of you who really strive, nor knoweth those (of you) who are steadfast?" (S. 3:142)

"That which befell you, on the day when the two armies met, was by permission of Allah; that He might know the true believers;" (S. 3:166)

"And that He might know the hypocrites, unto whom it was said: Come, fight in the way of Allah, or defend yourselves." (S. 3:167)

"O ye who believe! Allah will surely try you somewhat (in the matter) of the game which ye take with your hands and your spears, that <u>Allah may know</u> him who feareth Him in secret. Whoso transgresseth after this, for him there is a painful doom." (S. 5:94)

"Go, both of you, unto Pharaoh. Lo! he hath transgressed (the bounds). And speak unto him a gentle word, that <u>peradventure he may heed or fear</u>." (S. 20:43-44)

"And verily <u>We shall try you till We know</u> those of you who strive hard (for the cause of Allah) and the steadfast, and till We test your record." (S. 47:31)

"That <u>He may know</u> that they have indeed conveyed the messages of their Lord. He surroundeth all their doings, and He keepeth count of all things." (S. 72:28)

Objection # 12: *The Bible says God got tired and that's why he took a resting day! (Genesis 2:2) This cannot be the true description of God and therefore it is not from God.*

Response: First, the Bible makes it clear that God does not get tired or become weary: "*...The* LORD *is the everlasting God, the Creator of the ends of the earth. He will not grow tired (Hebrew:* יָעֵף*, yaw'af=to be fatigued, tired; to be fainted) or weary (Hebrew:* יָגַע*, yagah=to toil, labour; to be weary)...*" (Is.40:28). NIV

Second, the Bible never says God got tired. However, we read in Genesis chapter 2 verse 2:

"*By the seventh day God had finished the work he had been doing; so on the seventh day he <u>rested</u> (Hebrew:* בשׁת *Shabath) from all his work.*" (New International Version)

"*and God completeth by the seventh day His work which He hath made, and <u>ceaseth</u> (Hebrew:* שָׁבַת *Shabath) by the seventh day from all His work which He hath made.*" (Young's Literal Translation)

"*By the seventh day, God had completed the work he had been doing, so on the seventh day he <u>stopped</u> (Hebrew:* שָׁבַת *Shabath) working on everything that he had done.*" (International Standard Version)

From the above various translations we can see that the Bible is neither declaring nor implying that God gets tired and that's why He needs a day to rest! The translation nuances are misunderstood by some that way. The Hebrew word שָׁבַת 'shabath' means to desist; cease; rest; put an end to. Therefore, the plain meaning of the verse is after creating everything, God ceased from that action.

Objections # 13: *According to the Bible God orders Israelites to commit genocide i.e. to kill whole tribes and nations including children and animals (Num.31:1-47; Deut.25:17-19; Josh.6:15-21; 1Sam.15:1-35). This is unjust and cruel. God cannot be like this. Therefore the Bible is not God's word.*

Response: God by nature is holy and just. He doesn't overlook sin, but pours out His wrath both in this world and in the world to come on those who commit and perpetuate sin. In doing this God shows no partiality. He poured out His wrath even on His chosen people for the sins and abominations they had committed (Jud.20:1-48; 2King.8:11-13; Hosea 13:16).

God in His sovereignty is free to use *supernatural* or *natural* or *human* agencies to mete out His punishments on individuals, families or nations both in this world and in the world to come. The highest punishment an individual will have to endure is the punishment in Hell. This is what both Islam and Christianity teach. Do we call this cruelty? Absolutely not!

Example of supernatural agencies: The destruction of the cities Sodom and Gomorrah (Gen.19:1-29). Even in the Qur'an it is mentioned (S. 7:80-84). When these cities were destroyed apparently the little children, pregnant ladies and animals of those cities were also included in the destruction!

Example of natural agencies: The destruction of the people in the flood during Noah's time (Gen.7:1-24). The same is also mentioned in the Qur'an (S. 11:40-44). Again, apparently the little children, pregnant ladies and animals of that time were also included in the destruction! In fact, even today we see how the natural disasters such as earthquakes, tsunamis and epidemics of deadly diseases bring death and destruction to all, including good and bad, little and old, humans and animals. These take place under God's commands for reasons He alone knows.

Example of human agencies: The destruction of the Amalekites during Samuel's time (1Sam.151-35). Even in this God-sanctioned destruction of the Amalekites little children, pregnant ladies and animals were also included. Commands such as this are onetime or time-specific and context-specific in nature.

If innocent people, particularly children, become victims of God's wrath in the process God being perfectly just will certainly recompense all those innocent victims in the world to come to the fullest measure. In the light of these facts the above Muslim objection against the Bible becomes meaningless.

Objection # 14: *The Bible presents the holy prophet Jesus as an alcoholic drunkard.*
Response: Nothing could be further from the truth. Nowhere does the Bible say that Jesus Christ was a drunkard or drank alcoholic drink or fermented grape juice.

Wine in the Old Testament: (Hebrew: יין, yayin=wine, fermented grape juice)
a. Treated as a permissible drink (Gen.27:25; Eccl.9:7)
b. Forbidden in religious purification (Lev.10:9; Num.6:3)
c. Forbidden to people in authority (Prov.31:4)
d. Its abuse and excessive use for anyone forbidden (Prov.20:1; 21:17; 23:20)
e. Prescribed for people in pain and suffering (Prov.31:6-7)

Wine in the New Testament: (Greek: οἶνος, Oinos=fermented grape juice or unfermented grape juice)
a. Prescribed for medicinal use (1Tim.5:23)
b. Seeking its effect (drunkenness) forbidden (Eph.5:18)
c. Forbidden in religious purification (Lk.1:15)
d. Its abuse and excessive use forbidden (1Cor.5:11; 6:9-10)
e. Addiction to it is forbidden (1Tim.3:3, 8; Tit.2:3)

Jesus and wine:
a. The Bible never says that Jesus was drunk or even tasted wine i.e. fermented grape juice.
b. According to the Bible Jesus refused to drink wine even at the point of death (Mk.15:23).
c. The drink Jesus had at the last supper was unfermented grape juice for during that particular week Jews were ordered not to consume leavened bread or even have any leaven in their homes (Matt.26:27-29; Mk.14:23-25; Lk.22:17-18 cf. Ex.12:17-20,13:7).
d. In John chapter 2 we read about Jesus' first miracle of turning water into wine (Greek: οἶνος, Onios=fermented or unfermented grape juice). However, although the drink had the best taste of the 'wine' by God's power, it might not have had the ill effects of the wine or the fermented grape juice by the same power of God.

While the Qur'an forbids wine (fermented) and intoxicants without any exception, the Bible wisely forbids its misuse and prescribes it for medicinal purposes. This prescription is confirmed and made better use of by the modern medical sciences. Today, some medicines administered for various ailments contain alcohol. Ironically, even Muslims use them, particularly anesthetic drugs during operations or surgeries, which obviously go against the Qur'anic injunction and make them guilty in the light of Qur'anic teachings!

"The anti-bacterial nature of alcohol has long been associated with soothing stomach irritations and ailments like **traveler's diarrhea** where it was a preferred treatment to the less palatable bismuth treatments."
(http://en.wikipedia.org/wiki/Health_effects_of_wine)

For more information on the medicinal values of wine refer to the site http://www.medicalnewstoday.com/articles/265635.php

---

Questions to Muslims

"A similitude of the Garden which those who keep their duty (to Allah) are promised: Therein are rivers of water unpolluted, and rivers of milk whereof the flavour changeth not, and <u>rivers of wine delicious to the drinkers</u>, and rivers of clear-run honey; therein for them is every kind of fruit, with pardon from their Lord. (Are those who enjoy all this) like those who are immortal in the Fire and are given boiling water to drink so that it teareth their bowels?" (S. 47:15)

Question#1: If wine (the fermented grape juice) is forbidden strictly by the Qur'an in this world why does it promise rivers of wine (the fermented grape juice) in Islamic Paradise for the believers to enjoy?

Question#2: If you try to justify this by saying 'the wine in Paradise is not like the wine here on earth without any alcohol or its effects, then why didn't the Qur'an simply say 'in Paradise there will be rivers of grape juice' instead of rivers of wine?

****

"O ye who believe! <u>Draw not near unto prayer when ye are drunken, till ye know that which ye utter,</u> nor when ye are polluted, save when journeying upon the road, till ye have bathed. And if ye be ill, or on a journey, or one of you cometh from the closet, or ye have touched women, and ye find not water, then go to high clean soil and rub your faces and your hands (therewith). Lo! Allah is Benign, Forgiving." (S. 4:43)

Question#3: If wine and intoxicants are forbidden in Islam, why does the Qur'an say, *"Draw not near unto prayer when ye are drunken, till ye know that which ye utter"* which implies that it's ok to be drunk except during prayer time?

Scientific Problems

Accusation # 15: *It has scientific errors. Therefore it is not Allah's (God's) word.*
Response: Absolutely wrong. The Bible is not a systematic scientific manual. However, wherever it alludes to science it makes simple and accurate observations (Job.26:7,10; Prov.8:27; Is. 40:22; Lk.17:34-36; cf. S. 27:88; 15:19; 16:15; 78:6-7; 31:10; 21:31; 35:41). If one studies the Bible as it should be studied with the help of hermeneutic principles, then one cannot find even a single scientific error in it.

Question # 16: *In Genesis, we read that God created light which He called day, and separated it from the darkness which He called night (Genesis 1:3). Today we know that the alternation of day and night is caused by the earth's movement in relation to the sun. But, according to Genesis, the sun was not created until the fourth day (Genesis 1:16). So how could day and night alternate before that?*
Response: The Genesis account of creation in chapter one is a narrative from God's point of view. The very first verse has this to say:
"*In the beginning God created* (Hebrew: בָּרָא, bara = create out of nothing) *the heavens and the earth.*" (Genesis 1:1)

Points to notice:

a. Here we need to take notice of the word 'bara,' which refers to the creation act of God that brought creation out of nothing.
b. The heavens and the earth include the host of heaven and the earth in their essential make up.
c. God created all the above out of nothing.
d. This is the day one and at this stage the earth was formless and not yet fashioned into an inhabited planet.

Then we read,

"*Now the earth was formless and empty, darkness was over the surface of the* *deep, and the Spirit of God was hovering over the waters. And God said, "Let there be light," and there was light.* [4] *God saw that the light was good, and he separated the light from the darkness. God called the light "day," and the darkness he called "night." And there was evening, and there was morning—the first day* (Hebrew: יוֹם, *yowm* = time; day; year; period).*" (Genesis 1:2-5) NIV

Points to notice:

a. Earth came into existence, but was formless and empty. This resembles the way scientists describe the formation of the earth prior to acquiring a shape and climate that are suitable for the biological life to exist.
b. God created light out of nothing.
c. That was the first *yowm*. This could be a limited 24 hour day or a long period of time.
d. Since the system of 24 hour-day that results from the earth's movement in relation to the sun had not yet been in place, personally like many believing scientists I prefer to understand that it was a long period of time. I would also understand that all the six creation *yowms* may have been of different lengths of time, from twenty-four hour day to billions of years duration. God by His creative power could have created everything just in a twinkle of an eye. Yet, He chose to create in six separate *yowms*. Whether these *yowms* are literal 24 hour period we experience now or billions of years of periods like in the pre-historic times still they were appointed by God and what had happened in those *yowms* was the result of God's creative power.
e. The phrase 'evening and morning' in this context might be referring to the end of one *yowm* and the starting of another *yowm*.

"God made (Hebrew: עָשָׂה, *asah* = fashion; make; ordain; put in order) *two great lights—the greater light to govern the day and the lesser light to govern the night. He also made the stars. God set them in the vault of the sky to give light on the earth, to govern the day and the night, and to separate*

light from darkness. And God saw that it was good." (Genesis 1:16-18) NIV

Points to notice:

a. Here God did not create (*bara*), but made (*asah*) or formed or put together from that which had already been in existence.
b. The light that was already created had been assigned to these two bodies—sun and moon. Like in the case of a candle. Although a candle is in existence yet it doesn't give light until it is lighted with an external source of light.

In the light of the above observations we can understand that the phrase 'evening and morning' does not necessarily referring to the 24-hour 'day and night' period that we experience now as a result of the earth's movement in relation to the sun.

Objection # 17: *Vegetation is created on the third day (Genesis 1:11-12) whereas the sun which is necessary for sustaining vegetation does not appear until the fourth day (Genesis 1:16). This is a clear evidence for the scientific blunder in the Bible and therefore it is not from God.*
Response: Again, the conclusion is made on shallow understanding of the Scripture. According to the Bible the vegetation was created on the third day. But the light that was needed for the vegetation was already created on the first day:

"Now the earth was formless and empty, darkness was over the surface of the deep, and the Spirit of God was hovering over the waters. And God said, "Let there be light," and there was light. ⁴ God saw that the light was good, and he separated the light from the darkness. God called the light "day," and the darkness he called "night." And there was evening, and there was morning—the first day (Hebrew: יוֹם, *yowm* = time; day; year; period)." (Genesis 1:2-5) NIV

The light that was created on the first day was not yet assigned to the Sun which was put together (Hebrew: עָשָׂה, *asah* = fashion; make; ordain; put in order) only on the fourth day (Like in the case of a candle, although a candle is in existence yet it doesn't give light until it is lighted with an external source of light).

Question # 18: *The Bible mentions that the sun goes down or travels or lives in the sky (eg.Deut.11:30; Ps.19:4-6). This is completely against what the modern science teaches. Therefore, the Bible does contain scientific errors, which confirm that it is not God's word.*
Answer: When one ignores the hermeneutical principles while studying the Bible that's how one might end up thinking. The Bible used literary genres such as colloquialism and poetry. Even today in our conversations we use phrase like 'sun down' or 'sun rise.' Do we mean them literally? No! To point to west we say 'towards sun setting' or to east we say 'towards sun rising.'

"As you know, these mountains are across the Jordan, westward, toward the setting sun, near the great trees of Moreh, in the territory of those Canaanites living in the Arabah in the vicinity of Gilgal." (Deuteronomy 11:30) NIV

In the above verse the phrase 'toward the setting sun' simply means 'westward' in colloquial language. Likewise, below we see the description of the sun given in one of the Psalms. The Psalms in the Bible are songs written in poetic language to worship and glorify God. Poetry should be understood as poetry, but not as prose. Likewise, prose should be understood as prose, but not as poetry. A poem may describe the heart of a person as 'a hardened rock' or 'a melted cheese.' Do we take them as a literal hard rock or melted cheese? Of course, not! No one who knows how to read poetic literature would take everything in the following verses as literal as in a prose.

"Yet their voice goes out into all the earth, their words to the ends of the world. In the heavens God has pitched a tent for the sun.
It is like a bridegroom coming out of his chamber, like a champion rejoicing to run his course.
It rises at one end of the heavens and makes its circuit to the other; nothing is deprived of its warmth." (Psalm 19:4-6) NIV

> ### Question to Muslims
>
> **Question:** If you think the Holy Bible is wrong in employing poetic imagery, then how do you explain about the following Qur'anic teaching that sun sets in a muddy pool of water?
>
> *"Until, when he reached the setting of the sun, he found it set in a spring of murky water: Near it he found a People: We said: "O Zul-qarnain! (thou hast authority,) either to punish them, or to treat them with kindness."* (S. 18:86)

Problems of discrepancies

Let's begin with few typical arguments Muslims would bring in their discussions with Christians against the Holy Bible:

Dialogue # 1

Muslim: Hi Christian, your Bible is wrong for it's changed, has errors, contradictions etc.
Christian: Really?! Have you ever read the Holy Bible?
Muslim: Oh yes!
Christian: You mean you've read the whole of the Holy Bible?
Muslim: Well, not really. But I've read many parts of it.
Christian: If someone tells you without even reading the Qur'an fully once that the Qur'an is a false book and has many discrepancies in it, what would you think of him? Is that person a wise man or a fool, according to you?
Muslim: Well, such a person will definitely be a fool!
Christian: Why can't I think of you in the same way!
Muslims: ??!@#$%??

Dialogue # 2

Muslim: Hi Christian, do you think the Bible is God's word?
Christian: Yes, of course! Why did you ask that basic question?
Muslim: You should know that the Qur'an is truly God's word and that's why thousands of Muslims all over the world memorized it fully in the original Arabic language. This is not the case with the Bible. Can you show me one single Christian who memorized the
whole Bible?
Christian: Well, if that is the criterion for the authenticity of God's word I have some questions to ask you. First, tell me have you yourself memorized the whole Qur'an in original Arabic?

Muslim: Oops! Not really. But I know there are many Muslims who memorized it.
Christian: I am not asking about others, about you. Speak for yourself first. So you are a Muslim but you haven't memorized it, right?
Muslim: Yes, that's true. But memorizing the whole Qur'an in the original Arabic is not commanded for all Muslims to do, though.
Christian: Very good. So some Muslims do certain things like memorizing the whole Qur'an in original Arabic language despite the fact that the Qur'an doesn't command them to do. Don't you think that those Muslim are doing something against the Qur'an by memorizing it and then become proud about it?
Muslim: That's a good point. But I don't think all of them become proud of that.
Christian: Well, if not all at least some do, I guess! Such people in effect commit shirk. In any case, just because people memorized the whole Qur'an doesn't make it God's word. There are other religious books that were/are memorized by people. Ramayan, Mahabharatha, Geetha, Manas are some of them. Do you accept by your own standard that these books are also from Allah?
Muslim: Oh no. I don't.
Christian: The Holy Bible is from the one true God. It is three times bigger than the Qur'an. Revealed by God through several true prophets, priests, kings and apostles. If God commands us in the Bible that Christians must memorize it wholly in some language, then we would do that. Moreover, the most important thing is not to memorize God's word in its entirety, but to obey its teachings.
Muslim: You are right. I see the point.
Christian: One more thing. If some humans can memorize the whole Qur'an that only demonstrates to us how powerful the human brains created by God are over the Qur'an. I can argue saying that the Holy Bible is so powerful and that's why no human brain can memorize it wholly in any human language!

Accusation # 19: *The Bible contains changes, contradictions, errors and mistakes. This is a proof that the Bible is not from God.*
Response: This accusation is the result of ignorance or irrational thinking on the part of Muslims who make such accusations against the Bible! The fact of the matter is that the Bible as God's word doesn't contain any changes, contradictions, errors or mistakes.

(a) Changes. Theoretically it is possible to have changes in *some* of the manuscript copies and translations of the Bible which were made by fallible human beings who were not the inspired prophets or apostles. But this is hardly an evidence to say that all the translations and copies of the Bible contain changes from their originals! In order to say with absolute certainty that the current Bible or all the manuscripts of the Bible that we have today have changes from their originals, one must produce the original manuscripts to compare with in order to ascertain the changes. Since there are no such original manuscripts that differ from today's Bible all accusations of changes in the Bible are baseless and unfounded.

Interestingly, even in the seventh century Arabia during the Islamic prophet Muhammad's time there were many Jews and Christians in *Hijaz* (western Saudi Arabia) who had the Bible (Tawrarat, Zaboor and Injeel) in their possession according to the Islamic sources. Here are some examples:

"Those who follow the Messenger (Mohammed), the Prophet who can neither read nor write, whom they will find described in the Torah and the Gospel (which are) <u>with them.</u>" (Qur'an Sura 7:157)

> "Narrated 'Abdullah bin 'Umar: The Jews came to Allah's Apostle and told him that a man and a woman from amongst them had committed illegal sexual intercourse. Allah's Apostle said to them, "What do you find in the Torah (old Testament) about the legal punishment of Ar-Rajm(stoning)?" They replied, (But) we announce their crime and lash them." Abdullah bin Salam said, "You are telling a lie; Torah contains the order of Rajm." <u>They brought and opened the Torah</u> and one of them solaced his hand on the Verse of Rajm and read the verses preceding and following it. Abdullah bin Salam said to him, "Lift your hand." When he lifted his hand, the Verse of Rajm was written there. They said, "Muhammad has told the truth; the Torah has the Verse of Rajm. The Prophet then gave the order that both of them should be stoned to death. 'Abdullah bin 'Umar said, "I saw the man leaning over the woman to shelter her from the stones.""" (*Hadith Sahih Bukhari*: Volume 4, book 56, number 829.)

"Narrated Abdullah Ibn Umar: A group of Jews came and invited the Apostle of Allah (peace_be_upon_him) to Quff. So he visited them in their school. They said: AbulQasim, one of our men has committed fornication with a woman; so pronounce judgment upon them. They placed a cushion for the Apostle of Allah (peace_be_upon_him) who sat on it and said: Bring the Torah. It was then brought. He then withdrew the cushion from beneath him and placed the Torah on it saying: I believed in thee and in Him Who revealed thee. He then said: Bring me one who is learned among you. Then a young man was brought. The transmitter then mentioned the rest of the tradition of stoning similar to the one transmitted by Malik from Nafi' (*Hadith Sunan Abu Dawud*: Book 38, Number 4434 and 4431)."

"Khadija then accompanied him to her cousin Waraqa bin Naufal bin Asad bin 'Abdul 'Uzza, who, during the Pre-Islamic Period became a Christian and used to write the writing with Hebrew letters. He would write from the Gospel in Hebrew as much as Allah wished him to write…" (Hadith Sahih Al-Bukhari: Volume 1, Book 1, Number 3 & Volume 6, Book 60, Number 478)

Today's Bibles are taken from the copies that were made in the first six centuries of the Common Era and those copies still exist today. If today's Bible (Tawraat&Zaboor/Old Testament and Gospel/Injeel) is different from the seventh century Tawraat, Zaboor and Injeel which were approved by the Islamic prophet Muhammad why can't Muslims today show us at least one copy, in contrast to the thousands of copies of Tawraat and Injeel that we have today from the first five centuries alone, that confirms the so-called changes of the Bible that Muslims talk about? This shouldn't be an impossible task for Muslims to accomplish, if such a differing copy ever existed, given the fact that most of the Jews and Christians of seventh century in Hijaz (a region in the west of present-day Saudi Arabia) were either expelled, converted to Islam or killed and had their possessions, including their Bibles, confiscated by Muslims.

It is quite possible for some errors to creep into some of the copies and translations, but not necessarily into all the thousands of manuscripts we have today. This is where we must be mindful of the divine protection and supervision to the transmission as well as the preservation of God's word that is intended for mankind forever.

(b) *Contradictions.* Not necessarily everything that doesn't fit into our finite minds or make sense to our limited understanding is a contradiction. *A contradiction occurs when two or more mutually exclusive or conflicting statements are made with regard to an entity or event or scenario or subject in the same sense and for the same period of time.*

For example, here are two different statements: 'I saw my parents on January 1, 2014' and 'I did not see my parents on January 1, 2014.' These two statements are made about the same parents for the same period of time. They are mutually exclusive and therefore conflicting with each other. Two mutually exclusive statements made in the same sense referring to the same period of time cannot both be true. They are truly contradictory! However, there may be two or more statements that are different, but not mutually exclusive. Here is an example: 'I saw my parents on January 1, 2014,' and 'I saw my mother on January 1, 2014,' and 'I saw my father on January 1, 2014.' These three statements are different, but not mutually exclusive and are therefore not conflicting with each other. They all can be true in the same sense and for the same period of time. These three statements are different from one another, yet they do not form real contradiction.

There may be apparent but not actual contradictions in the contents of the Bible. Upon close examination of the alleged contradictions in the Bible an honest seeker can realize that those so-called contradictions are not real contradictions at all. It has been established that the Bible does not contain even a single *real* contradiction in it.

For more than two thousand years critiques have been trying with all their power to prove contradictions in the Bible, but without success. All that they succeeded in their efforts so far is to point out the problems that exist in some imperfect translations or manuscript copies! What does it prove? The translators and the copyists are fallible, not the word of God itself!

Objection # 20: *The Bible says in one place animals were created first and then humans (Gen.1:25-26). In another place, however, it says that first* *humans were created and after that beasts (Gen.2:18-19). This is a clear contradiction. Therefore it is not from Allah (God).*

Response: Yes, as we see in Genesis 1:25-26 God had created animals, livestock and all kinds of creatures on the ground, in the air and in water before He created mankind. Nowhere in the Bible do we read that 'God created animals after He had created mankind.' The fact is that first God created animals and later mankind. The same thing can also be expressed as, 'God created mankind after He had created animals' or 'God created mankind. God gave animals to mankind which He had already created.'

The account in Genesis 1:25-26 is not in conflict with the account in Genesis 2:18-19, except that the latter account presents the same information of the former account in a different way.

"The LORD God said, "It is not good for the man to be alone. I will make a helper suitable for him." Now the <u>LORD God had formed</u> out of the ground all the wild animals and all the birds in the sky. <u>He brought them</u> to the man to see what he would name them; and whatever the man called each living creature, that was its name." (Gen.2:18-19) NIV

The LORD God brought the animals, which He had already created, to the man in order for him to be able to name them. There is no contradiction in these verses of the Bible. The perceived so-called contradiction mentioned in the objection is only in the translations, but not in the original language text of the Scriptures.

Objections # 21: *The Bible says Saul fell on his own sword and died (1Sam.31:4-6). But the same Bible says that Saul was killed by another person (2Sam.1:6-10). Which of these two accounts is true? This proves that the Bible contains contradictions and therefore it is not from Allah (God).*

Response: In the above two places the Bible mentions the death of Saul. However, in the first place i.e. 1Sam.31:4-6, it giving the direct narration of the even, while in the second place i.e. 2Sam.1:6-10, it only reporting the narration of the events as related by the Amalekite. The narration of the death of Saul as given by the Amalekite could well be a lie. The Amalekite having known that Saul had hated David and David's life was in danger from Saul might have concocted the lie hoping to gain a favor from David.

In essence, the Bible is not giving two conflicting accounts about Saul's death. The failure to understand the contexts of the statements in the Bible is the reason behind the objection in this regard.

Objection # 22: *Which are the last words of Jesus, 'Eli, eli, lama sabacthani?' (Matt.27:46) or 'Father, unto thy hands I commend my spirit.' (Lk.23:46) or 'It is finished.' (Jn.19:30)? These are conflicting statements about Jesus' last words and therefore it is not from Allah (God).*
Response: Let's first see what the Bible says in these references.

"About the ninth hour Jesus cried out with a loud voice, saying, "ELI, ELI, LAMA SABACHTHANI?" that is, "MY GOD, MY GOD, WHY HAVE YOU FORSAKEN ME?...And Jesus cried out again with a loud voice, and yielded up His spirit." (Matt.27:46...50) NASB
"Therefore when Jesus had received the sour wine, He said, "It is finished!" And He bowed His head and gave up His spirit." (Jn.19:30) NASB
"And Jesus, crying out with a loud voice, said, "Father, INTO YOUR HANDS I COMMIT MY SPIRIT." Having said this, He breathed His last." (Lk.23:46) NASB

What we read in Matthew 27:46 are obviously not the last words of Jesus. Because, Jesus made another loud voice in verse 50, although it is not written there what He had said at that point, and then dies.

In John 19:30 we read about two different actions of Jesus, namely, He said "It is finished" and later He bowed His head in death. Between these two actions of Jesus what we read in Luke 23:46 has taken place. In essence, *"Father, INTO YOUR HANDS I COMMIT MY SPIRIT"* are the last words of Jesus on the cross before His death.

The above statements in the Bible are not conflicting with each other.

Question # 23: *The death of Judas Iscariot: 'It is written in Mathew 27:5 that Judas died by hanging himself, but in Acts 1:18 it is written that he died by falling headlong and bursting open with all his bowels gushing out. These are clear conflicting accounts and therefore they form real contradiction. This proves that the Bible does have contradictions and therefore it is not from God.'*

Answer: No, this is not a real contradiction. In the Bible we see two different accounts about Judas ending his life—
(1) *'And he threw the pieces of silver into the temple sanctuary and departed; and he went away and hanged himself.'* (Matthew 27:5) NASB
(2) *'Now this man acquired a field with the price of his wickedness, and falling headlong, he burst open in the middle and all his intestines gushed out.'* (Acts 1:18) NASB

But these above two statements are complementary statements rather than conflicting statements. It would be a contradiction, if the two statements in the Bible were like the following:
(1) And he threw the pieces of silver into the temple sanctuary and departed; and he went home and hanged himself and died on the spot.
(2) Now this man acquired a field with the price of his wickedness and falling headlong from a cliff, he burst open in the middle and all his intestines gushed out and as a result of that he died.

These are two mutually exclusive statements. These statements both cannot be true. That's why here we can see a real contradiction. But these statements are not from the Bible!

The actual two statements from the Bible are not mutually exclusive and conflicting, rather they are complimentary. In the first statement we see that Judas hanged himself. But it doesn't explicitly say that he died at that point. It also doesn't say anything about the place where it occurred. The second statement says about Judas' fall and what happened to his body in the process of that fall. However, it doesn't say anything explicitly about his death or the place where his fall had occurred. If we put the information from these two statements together we can easily construct the full story behind Judas' suicidal death. Some Bible scholars concluded that after Judas had felt remorse he went to the 'Ben Hinnom valley' which is near Jerusalem and hanged himself on a tree that was on the edge of the valley.

Soon after he hanged himself on one of the branches of the tree that were overlooking the valley, in all probability the branch on which he hanged himself broke off and he fell down into the valley along its ridges. By the time he hit the bottom of the valley Judas was headlong and burst open in the middle and all his intestines gushed out. He died either soon after he hanged himself or as he was falling down alongside the rugged ridge or when he finally hit the bottom of the valley. Regardless of the exact location of his death, he did die! The fact is that there is no conflict in the two different statements of the Bible regarding the end of Judas' life. The details were recorded from two different aspects, one about the former part and the other about the latter part of the incident. God's word doesn't have contradictions!

Question # 24: *According to the Bible the chief priests took Judas money and bought Potter's field as a burial field for strangers (Matthew 27:3-8). But the same Bible says that it was Judas himself who bought the field (Acts 1:15-19). These two accounts are contradictory and therefore cannot be true. This also proves that the Bible is not from Allah (God)*
Response: First let's see what the verses in question say.

"And they conferred together and with the money <u>bought</u> (Greek: ἀγοράζω, agorazo= to buy; to redeem) *the Potter's Field as a burial place for strangers."* (Matt.27:7) NASB

"Now this man <u>acquired</u> (Greek: κτάομαι, kataomai=to acquire; to procure) *a field with the price of his wickedness, and falling headlong, he burst open in the middle and all his intestines gushed out."* (Acts 1:18) NASB

From the above verses it is apparent that two different Greek words have been used in the above verses. They both differ in their meaning. The above verses would conflict if they say something like below:

1. *And they conferred together <u>after Judas death</u> and with the money bought...*
2. *Now this man <u>bought</u>...*

But in reality the Bible does not contain the above two sentences that would amount to a contradiction. Besides, in all probability when Judas' threw the money into the sanctuary (Matt.27:5) the chief priests might have bought the field immediately with the money that belongs to Judas before Judas committed suicide. In such a scenario, even though the field was purchased by the chief priests, yet it is considered Judas' as the money for the purchase belongs to him. This is what prompted Peter to say, *'this man acquired a field…'* (Acts 1:18)

Question # 25: *The Bible mentions in one place that humans cannot see God (Jn.1:18) and in another place it mentions that some humans did see God (Gen.32:30). It's a contradiction therefore it's not from God.*

Answer: As has been mentioned in the chapter 'Christian position on God's word,' no human being can see God in His full eternal glory and form. However, God in His grace allowed some chosen people to see Him in a veiled and temporal form.

Objections # 26: *The genealogy of Jesus according to Matthew testifies that the father of Joseph was Jacob. But the genealogy of Jesus according to Luke reports that the father of Joseph was Heli. It's a clear contradiction. One person cannot be the son of two different persons. Therefore the Bible is not from Allah (God).*

Answer: No, that's not a contradiction at all. For it to be a contradiction we should read in the Bible 'Joseph was the son of Jacob' and also 'Joseph was not the son of Jacob.' A person first is the son of his or her biological father and later can become the son or daughter of a stepfather or a foster father or an adopted father. Or sometimes the name of the father could be given only in part in one place and the other part in other place. For example, a person whose name is 'Jacob Heli' can be the father of Joseph, even though we are told that Joseph is the son of Jacob in one place and the son of Heli in another place.

In the original Greek manuscript copies of the genealogy of Jesus given in Luke we don't see the sentence 'Joseph was the son of Heli.' In the entire genealogy account given by Luke the word 'son' (Gk: υἱός, huios) in the original Greek language is not used except once in the very beginning i.e. in verse 23. Even there too it only alludes to the adopted sonship of Jesus to Joseph.

Heli the father of Mary as confirmed in the extra biblical historical accounts seemed to have only daughters—Mary and her sister (cf.Jn.19:25). Like in many Eastern cultures in the ancient Jewish culture when a man doesn't have a son but only daughters, then his daughters and their husbands (sons-in-law) would ultimately become his heirs (cf.Num.26:33, 27:4-7). Apparently that's what had happened in the case of Heli and his son-in-law Joseph. This is why Luke traces Jesus' genealogy through David's son Nathan to Heli and then to Joseph. This way Joseph is not the literal son of Heli just like Jesus being called as Joseph's son or Adam being called as God's son in the same genealogy given by Luke.

Objections # 27: *According to Luke Simon of Cyrene was the person who carried the cross (Lk.23:26). But according to John it was Jesus who carried the cross (Jn.19:17). Which one of these two is true? Since the Bible contains this contradictions it's not from Allah (God).*
Response: Let's see how the Bible records these events.

"As the soldiers led him away, they seized Simon from Cyrene, who was on his way in from the country, and put the cross on him and made him carry it behind Jesus." (Lk.23:26) NIV
"Carrying his own cross, he went out to the place of the Skull (which in Aramaic is called Golgotha)." (Jn.19:17) NIV

In Luke 23:26 we read that Simon of Cyrene carried the cross behind Jesus. However, how long he carried the cross the verse doesn't say. It could be that he carried the cross to some distance, but later Jesus took it on to himself and carried it to the end as we read in John 19:17. No contradiction is found between these two verses.

Objections # 28: *According to Mark Mary Magdalene visited the tomb of Jesus after sunrise (Mark16:1-2), but according to Matthew, Luke and John she came there before sunrise (Matt.28:1-2, Lk.24:1-2, Jn.20:1).*

Which of these two accounts is true? Since the Bible contains these two conflicting accounts it's not from Allah (God).
Response: Let's fist see all the verses that talk about Mary Magdalene's visit to the tomb.

"After the Sabbath, <u>at dawn</u> on the first day of the week, Mary Magdalene and the other Mary went to look at the tomb." (Matt.28:1) NIV
"When the Sabbath was over, Mary Magdalene, Mary the mother of James, and Salome bought spices so that they might go to anoint Jesus' body. Very early on the first day of the week, <u>just after sunrise</u>, they were on their way to the tomb." (Mk.16:1-2) NIV
"On the first day of the week, <u>very early in the morning</u>, the women took the spices they had prepared and went to the tomb." (Lk.24:1-2) NIV
"Early on the first day of the week, <u>while it was still dark</u>, Mary Magdalene went to the tomb and saw that the stone had been removed from the entrance." (Jn.20:1) NIV

None of the above verses is talking about Mary Magdalene's visit to the tomb 'before sunrise.' Her visit was 'at dawn' (according to Matthew), 'just after sunrise' (according to Mark), 'very early in the morning' (according to Luke), and 'while it was still dark' (according to John). The tomb was surrounded by trees as it was located in the midst of a garden. In all likelihood, the women – including Mary Magdalene – woke up early that day and started their journey. However, by the time they reached the tomb, due to surrounding trees, morning clouds and nearby hills the place was 'still dark' although it was just 'after the sunrise' which is basically 'at the dawn' or 'very early in the morning.'

In summary, all the above accounts are true and none of them contradicts others.

Objection # 29: *In one place the Bible says Elijah ascended into heaven (2King.2:1). In another place the same Bible says no one ascended into haven except the Son of Man (Jn.3:13). Which one of these two conflicting statements is true? Since the Bible contains this contradiction it cannot be from Allah (God).*
Response: In John 3:13 the words of Jesus are part of a lengthy discourse with the Jewish leader Nicodemus. This discourse starts

at verse 1 and ends at 21. In order to understand the actual meaning of the verse 13 we need to take the whole context into consideration. The preceding verses would shed the light needed to grasp its intended meaning.

"*¹¹Very truly I tell you, we speak of what we know, and we testify to what we have seen, but still you people do not accept our testimony. ¹² I have spoken to you of earthly things and you do not believe; how then will you believe if I speak of heavenly things? ¹³ No one has ever gone into heaven except the one who came from heaven—the Son of Man.*" (Jn.3:11-13) NIV

In his discourse with Nicodemus, Jesus is talking about spiritual matters that Nicodemus found difficult to accept. At this point Jesus spoke to him something like this:

"Nicodemus, I am telling you what I have seen. Until now, I have only spoken to you about earthly things, yet you are finding it difficult to understand. If I tell you about heavenly things, which I have seen, you cannot believe. I can tell you heavenly things also because I have been to Heaven; in fact, I came from there. No one in this world (in our generation) could tell you heavenly things like I do, because no one (in our generation) has been to heaven like me."

Had Jesus meant that no one at any time, including Enoch and Elijah, has ever ascended into Heaven, then Nicodemus being a religious Jew who knew about what had happened to Enoch and Elijah would have corrected Jesus immediately. Since Nicodemus understood Jesus' words properly in their context he did not venture to find fault with Jesus' statement. The two statements in the Bible are not conflicting with each other.

Objection # 30: *The Bibles says in some places that God is changeless (1Sam.15:29; Mal.3:6) and in other places God changed (Gen.6:6; Jon.3:10). This is a clear contradiction in the Bible and therefore it is not from Allah (God).*
Response: Let's see what the Bible says in this respect.

"And also the Strength of Israel will not lie nor repent (Heb:*nacham*,נָחַם=to be sorry; have compassion; to repent); *for he is not a man, that he should repent."* (1Sam.15:29) ASV

"I the LORD *do not change* (Hebrew: *nacham*,נָחַם=to be sorry; have compassion; to repent). *So you, the descendants of Jacob, are not destroyed."* (Mal.3:6) NIV

"The LORD *was sorry* (Hebrew: *nacham*,נָחַם=to be sorry; have compassion; to repent) *that He had made man on the earth, and He was grieved in His heart."* (Gen.6:6) NASB

"Then God saw their actions—that they had turned from their evil ways—so God relented (Hebrew: *nacham*,נָחַם=to be sorry; have compassion; to repent) *from the disaster He had threatened to do to them. And He did not do it."* (Jon.3:10) HCSB

Firstly, in the above verses the Hebrew word 'nacham' is used with different meanings. Like Arabic words Hebrew words also carry several different meanings. Usually, context determines the meaning of a word. As we can see from the above translations the Hebrew word 'nacham' is used with different meaning in different verses. To insist on only one meaning to this word at every place it appears in the Bible is not only unscholarly but also childish.

Secondly, there can never be a change in God's nature and essence. However, God's actions such as His plans, His dealings with people, and instructions He gives to mankind can change. These changes neither imply nor necessitate change in God's nature or essence.

Finally, in 1Sam.15:29 and Mal.3:6 God is contrasting Himself with human beings who are fickle minded in the decisions they take and are prone to lie in the statements they make. In so doing God is assuring us that His decisions are meaningful and appropriate, and His statements are truthful and dependable.

In the light of these facts the so-called contradiction evaporates into thin air!

Question to Muslims

Question: Dear Muslims, if you have objections to the God of the Bible in changing His plans or instructions or dealings don't you think the same objections are also applicable to the Quranic Allah as we see his changes in the Quran?

Example#1
In Mecca Muhammad gave the 'revelation,' "*There is no compulsion in religion.*" (S.2:256)
But in Medina he gave another 'revelation' differing from the above, "*O ye who believe! Fight those of the disbelievers who are near to you, and let them find harshness in you, and know that Allah is with those who keep their duty (unto Him).*" (S.9:123)

Example#2
First Muhammad gave the punishment for adulterers as life imprisonment through a 'revelation,' "*As for those of your women who are guilty of lewdness, call to witness four of you against them. And if they testify (to the truth of the allegation) then confine them to the houses until death take them or (until) Allah appoint for them a way.*" (S.4:15)
Later he changed the punishment to flogging with 100 strokes through another 'revelation,' "*The adulterer and the adulteress, scourge ye each one of them (with) a hundred stripes. And let not pity for the twain withhold you from obedience to Allah, if ye believe in Allah and the Last Day. And let a party of believers witness their punishment.*" (S.24:2)

(c) ***Errors or mistakes.*** For those who know how to read and study the Bible there are no errors or mistakes in the Bible. But for those who do not know how to read and study the Bible there appears to be numerous errors and mistakes in it!

As explained in the previous pages, once the contents of the Bible are examined in their proper contexts and original language genres, devices, techniques and phrases the so-called errors or mistakes disappear. Here are some examples—

Question # 31: *What is described in Matthew 27:9-10 is a quote from what prophet Zechariah wrote in Zechariah 11:12-13. Yet, the Bible says, "Then that which was spoken through* Jeremiah *the prophet was fulfilled..." (Matt.27:9). This is a clear mistake made by the writer of the Gospel according to Matthew. Therefore, the Bible is not God's word for it contains mistakes.*

Response: No, this is not a mistake. Some people might think that Matthew 27:9-10 is a quotation from Zechariah 11:12-13. However, this is not necessarily the case. If we compare both quotes it becomes apparent that these two are not same for there is very little common between them:

"Then what was spoken by Jeremiah the prophet was fulfilled: "They took the <u>thirty pieces of silver</u>, the price set on him by the people of Israel, and they used them to buy the potter's field, as the Lord commanded me." (Matthew 27:9-10) NIV

"I told them, "If you think it best, give me my pay; but if not, keep it." So they paid me <u>thirty pieces of silver</u>. And the LORD said to me, "Throw it to the potter"—the handsome price at which they valued me! So I took the thirty pieces of silver and threw them to the potter at the house of the LORD." (Zechariah 11:12-13) NIV

In the above two quotes we see only the phrase 'thirty pieces of silver' common to both. Based on this one cannot conclude that what was mentioned in Mathew 27:9-10 is the same as what was written in Zechariah 11:12-13. The common phrase we see in both quotes is only an accidental occurrence. Therefore, Matthew is not quoting Zechariah. However, as Matthew mentions in verse 9 it's a fulfilment of what prophet Jeremiah *spoke*. Does that mean it should be mentioned in the Old Testament book of Jeremiah? Not necessarily.

Of course, if the verse says, 'Then what was *written* by Jeremiah the prophet was fulfilled,' only then we should expect to find it in the book of Jeremiah. However, in Matthew 27:9 we read that 'what was **spoken** by Jeremiah,' but not 'what was ***written*** by Jeremiah.' Besides, not necessarily every single word that the prophets had uttered or prophesied was preserved in written form. Eg. Jn.21:25; Jude 14-15. The Bible doesn't contain errors or mistakes!

Question # 32: *In Matthew 23:35 Jesus says, "And so upon you will come all the righteous blood that has been shed on earth, from the blood of righteous Abel to the blood of Zechariah son of Berekiah, whom you murdered between the temple and the altar." Here Jesus referred to 2Chronicles 24:20-21. While the father of Zechariah was Jehoiada the priest in the O.T., Jesus* *says 'the blood of Zechariah son of Berekiah' in the N.T. It's an obvious mistake made by Jesus, according to the Bible. This shows the Bible contains mistakes.*

Response: Reference Bibles provide cross-referencing passages to assist us in our study of the Bible. Even in this case, several Bibles link Matthew 23:35 with 2 Chronicles 24:20-21. Although we see several similarities in these two accounts, upon close scrutiny it becomes apparent that these two are separate accounts. Similarity does not necessarily mean sameness.

- The Zechariah son of Jehoiada was killed *'in the court of the house of the LORD.'* Whereas the Zechariah Jesus mentioned was *'murdered between the temple and the altar.'* These are two different locations.

- The Zechariah son of Jehoiada was killed around 700 B.C. However, Jesus was referring to all the killings of the righteous people from the beginning to the end of the O.T.

- The Zechariah son of Jehoiada (Chro.24:20) is different from the Zechariah son of Berechiah (Zech.1:1) the prophet who lived towards the end of the O.T. period i.e. 520 B.C. Jesus, in reality, was referring to this Zechariah the prophet.

- The Zechariah son of Jehoiada was not the descendant of Iddo. Whereas the Zechariah son of Berechiah was the descendant of Iddo (Zech.1:1). This Zechariah was both prophet and priest during his ministry.

- Although the murder of the prophet Zechariah is not recorded in the Bible, Jews were aware of that incident that is why Jesus mentioned it to the Jews he was addressing. From historic point of view we can see that even the Jewish Targum makes mention of it: *"The Attribute of Justice replied, and said, "Is it right to <u>kill priest and prophet in the Temple of the LORD</u>, as when you <u>killed Zechariah son of Iddo,</u> the High Priest and faithful prophet in the Temple of the LORD on the Day of Atonement because he admonished you not to do evil before the LORD?"* (English translation by C.M.M. Brady at http://www.targum.info/meg/tglam.htm,Targum 2:20). The Hebrew phrase 'son of' can also mean 'descendant of.'

Again, the Bible doesn't contain errors or mistakes!

Question # 33: *Did Jesus die on the tree or stake (Acts 5:30, 10:39) or cross (Matthew 27:42; Mark 15:30; John 19:25)?*
Response: This confusion is caused due to translation nuances and language limitations.

"If someone guilty of a capital offense is put to death and their body is exposed on a pole, you must not leave the body hanging on the pole overnight. Be sure to bury it that same day, because anyone who is hung on a pole (Hebrew: עֵץ ets = wood; tree; timber; stick) is under God's curse. You must not desecrate the land the LORD *your God is giving you as an inheritance."* (Deuteronomy 21:22-23) NIV

The above verse is from the O.T. It clearly says that a person who is accursed should be hung on an 'ets.' Here the Hebrew word 'ets' can mean a stick or a wooden pole or a tree. Wood is common in all these. If a person is hung on a wooden door or a wooden bridge it still amounts to the same meaning i.e. he is accursed.

With this understanding if we turn to the N.T. there we see that Jesus was killed on 'something.' Now let's study the Scriptures to see what that 'something' was.

""He saved others," they said, "but he can't save himself! He's the king of Israel! Let him come down now from the cross (Greek: σταυρός, stauros = upright stake; cross or Roman instrument of the most cruel and ignominious punishment), and we will believe in him." (Matthew 27:42) NIV
"Come down from the cross (Greek: σταυρός, stauros) and save yourself!" (Mark 15:30) NIV
"Near the cross (Greek: σταυρός, stauros) of Jesus stood his mother, his mother's sister, Mary the wife of Clopas, and Mary Magdalene." (John 19:25) NIV

Romans killed Jesus upon Jewish insistence. The cruelest form of punishment the Romans of the first century used was 'cross.' The Encyclopedia Americana, Volume 8, 2000 edition, p. 260 affirms this:

History of Crucifixion as Capital Punishment. Crucifixion was used as a form of capital punishment from about the 6th century B.C. to the 4th century A.D. It probably originated among the Persians, from whom it spread to other peoples such as the EGYPTIANS, Carthaginians, and Romans. Crucifixion was not inflicted on Roman citizens, but only on slaves and subject peoples. In 337, it was banned by Constantine the Great out of respect for Jesus Christ, who suffered death on the cross at the hands of the Roman rulers of Palestine.

However, the N.T. mentions this differently as we see in the following verses:

"We ourselves are witnesses of everything He did in both the Judean country and in Jerusalem, yet they killed Him by hanging Him on a tree (Greek: ξύλον, *xylon* = wood; tree; anything made of wood).*"* (Acts 10:39) (HCSB)

"Christ has redeemed us from the curse of the law by becoming a curse for us, because it is written: Everyone who is hung on a tree (Greek: ξύλον, *xylon*) *is cursed."* (Galatians 3:13) HCSB

Do the above two verses contradict with the fact that Jesus was crucified on a cross that was made with two wooden beams? No, not at all! 'Xylon' (wooden beams) is anything that is made of wood. In that sense even 'stauros' (cross) is also a 'xylon.'

"So the other disciples kept telling him, "We have seen the Lord!" But he said to them, "If I don't see the mark of the nails (Greek: ἧλος, *helos* = nails) *in His hands, put my finger into the mark of the nails, and put my hand into His side, I will never believe!"* (John 20:25) HCSB

In the above verse Thomas one of Jesus' disciples told the other disciples that he would not believe that Jesus was resurrected unless he sees '*the mark of the* **nails** *in His hands.*' Had Jesus got crucified on a pole or a single stake, then Thomas would have to say, 'the mark of the nail,' which he did not. Thomas' statement confirms the fact that Jesus has had the marks of two nails - one in each hand - for He was crucified on two crossed-beams like a cross but not on a single pole as the false teachers Jehovah's Witnesses believe and teach.

In summary, Jesus died on a cross that was made of wood that came from a tree!

Question # 34: *The Bible says in one place that Jesus was crucified at third hour and later the same Bible says that it was at sixth hour (Mark 15:25; John 19:14-16). Therefore, it cannot be from God.*
Response: If we understand the context and the way time was reckoned in different contexts as given in different books then the discrepancy disappears.

"It was the third hour when they crucified Him." (Mark 15:25) NASB
"Now it was the day of preparation for the Passover; it was about the sixth hour. And he said to the Jews, "Behold, your King!... So he then handed Him over to them to be crucified." (John 19:14...16) NASB

The Roman clock, or time of day, was divided into 12 hours (Latin *horae*) of light and 12 hours of darkness. The Roman civil and religious day began at midnight from a very early time. The hours of the day and the night were always counted from dusk, or dawn, hence that the "sixth hour" represented midnight or midday respectively.

Jewish day begins and ends at sundown. Each day is divided into four night watches or twelve hours and four day watches or twelve hours. The Jewish daytime hours begin with dawn and end with dusk.

Gospel according to Matthew, Mark and Luke follow the Jewish reckoning of time as they were primarily addressed the people who were of Jewish origin and living in and around Jewish land. When a person living in that context heard 'third hour' it simply meant to that person '9am of our time.'

However, the Gospel according to John was primarily addressed to the people living outside of Palestine who followed Roman reckoning of time that the whole world follows now. When a person living in this context hears 'sixth hour' it means to that person as 6am.

With this clarity now we can see that both John and Mark pointed to the same time i.e. 6am, when Jesus was tried and handed over to be crucified. Later, at 9am He was crucified outside of Jerusalem. From noon to 3pm there was darkness over the land and at about 3pm Jesus gave up His life. Shortly before 6pm that day His body was taken down from the cross to be kept in a sepulcher.

Question # 35: *The Bible says in one place that the people who accompanied Saul (Paul) did hear the voice from the vision he had (Acts 9:7) and in another place it says that they did not hear the voice from that vision (Acts 22:9). This is a contradiction and therefore it cannot be from Allah (God).*

Response: Let's see what the Bible actually recorded about this: "*The men traveling with Saul stood there speechless; they heard* (Greek: ἀκούω, akouo = to hear in various senses such as only as noise or comprehending the meaning) *the sound but did not see anyone.*" (Acts 9:7) NIV

"*My companions saw the light, but they did not* (Greek: οὐ, ou = not) *understand* (Greek: ἀκούω, akouo = to hear in various senses such as only as noise or comprehending the meaning) *the voice of him who was speaking to me.*" (Acts 22:9) NIV

In the above two different verses, the same Greek word 'akouo' is used, but with different meanings. In Acts 9:7 it denotes 'hearing just sound or noise without any understanding.' But in Acts 22:9 it denotes 'hearing the sound with understanding,' but with the combination of an absolute negative adverb in Greek 'ou' giving the same meaning as the earlier one. Usually the context determines the meaning of a word if it has several shades of meanings.

This Muslim objection is based on some unclear translations of the above verses. However, when we see its proper translation in New International Version the meaning becomes clear and the so-called contradiction disappears.

Question # 36: *The Bible says in one place Michal Saul's daughter had no children (2Samuel 6:23) and in another place it says Michal did have five children (2Samuel 21:8). It's a contradiction and therefore it's not from Allah (God).*

Response: This objection is based on the mistakes made by copyists in the manuscript copies. In 2Sam.21:8 not all the ancient manuscripts contain Michal's name. Although the majority manuscripts do contain 'Michal' in verse 2Sam.21:8 - a possible mistake that was carried on into many subsequent copies - some ancient manuscripts do contain 'Merab' Saul's first daughter's name in that verse. NIV translation makes this clear in its footnotes:

"*And Michal daughter of Saul had no children to the day of her death.*" (2Sam.6:23) NIV
"*But the king took Armoni and Mephibosheth, the two sons of Aiah's daughter Rizpah, whom she had borne to Saul, together with the five sons of Saul's daughter Merab,[a] whom she had borne to Adriel son of Barzillai the Meholathite.*" (2Sam.21:8) NIV

Footnotes:
  a. 2 Samuel 21:8 Two Hebrew manuscripts, some Septuagint manuscripts and Syriac (see also 1 Samuel 18:19); most Hebrew and Septuagint manuscripts *Michal*

Age of Ishmael when Abraham sent him away along with his mother Hagar

Objection # 37: *In Geneses the Bible says Hagar bore Abraham son Ishmael when Abraham was eighty-six years old (Gen.16:15-16). Later we are told that Sarah bore Abraham the promised son Isaac when Abraham was hundred years old (Gen.21:5). After sometime at Sarah's insistence Abraham sent Hagar and her son Isaac away. However, the Bible tells us that Ishmael was a small baby that Hagar carried and placed him under a bush as he was crying (Gen.21:9-21). This is a clear discrepancy regarding Ishmael's age in the Bible. Therefore it is not form God.*
Response: This is a case of Scriptures being misread and misinterpreted based on imperfect translations.

By the time Sarah bore the promised son Isaac to Abraham Hagar's son Ishmael was fourteen years old. When Isaac was about a year old child Hagar and her son Ishmael were sent out. By this time Ishmael had been a fifteen years old teenager. This is what the Bible says regarding how they were sent out:

"*Early the next morning Abraham took some food and a skin of water and gave them to Hagar. He set them on her shoulders and then sent her off with the boy* (Hebrew: יֶלֶד, yeled). *She went on her way and wandered in the Desert of Beersheba.*" (Gen.21:14) NIV

Points to notice:

a. Nowhere does the Bible say Abraham placed the boy (yeled) on Hagar's shoulder (Hebrew: יֶלֶד , yeled = boy; son; child; youth; young man). This is the word used in Genesis 21:14-16. However, Hebrew language has a different word for a small child or an infant that mothers need to carry i.e. olal (Hebrew: עוֹלָל, olal = babe; small child; little child; infant. Eg. 1Samuel 15:3; Hosea 13:16). This is not the word that is used in Genesis 21:14-16!

b. Even Joseph in his late teens was referred to as 'yeled' (boy) in the Bible (Eg. Genesis 42:22).

c. The boy Ishmael was around fifteen years old by this time.

d. Abraham placed food and water, but not necessarily Ishmael, on Hagar's shoulders. Ishmael was not a small child anymore.

e. Abraham sent Hagar off with Ishmael.

f. Hagar wandered with Ishmael, not in a garden nor even in the shades of a green forest, but in the Beersheba desert which is located in the south-west part of Israel.

g. Beersheba desert is a hot sun-scorching place where temperatures sometimes rise to 50 degree Celsius. Being a desert land it is frequented with bushes rather than trees.

h. No mother would leave a 'small child' under a bush and expects to see his death when the 'small child' simply cries for water!

i. Apparently while wandering in the Beersheba desert the boy (yeled) Ishmael became exhausted and got incapacitated due to sunstroke in that sun-scorching desert. It is in this condition that his mother Hagar leaves Ismael under a bush and begins to wonder that he was going to die.

In a place like Beersheba desert even a fifteen year old boy can easily become dehydrated in a matter of hours. In all likelihood Ishmael had sunstroke and was dehydrated and became weak like a small child. Those who have seen persons in similar conditions can easily imagine Ishmael's condition. The fact that Hagar did not try to breast-feed him at that point also confirms that Ishmael was not a small child at that time. It is common knowledge that sunstroke or dehydration can make even older people like infants in terms of their physical strength and movements. This is the perfect explanation of the fifteen year old Ishmael's condition in the desert in the Biblical narrative. That is why his mother Hagar might have carried him some distance but finally when her strength too failed she places him under a bush assuming that he was going to die.

There is no discrepancy in the age of Ishmael in the Bible. When we understand the context and text of the Bible properly then the supposed contradiction evaporates into thin air!

JESUS CURSING THE FIG TREE

Objection # 37: *Jesus was hungry and went to a fig tree looking for something to eat (Matthew 21:18-20; Mark 11:12-14, 20-21). When he saw that there were no figs on the tree he cursed it. Regarding this same incident there is a discrepancy between Matthew's account and Mark's account. Mathew says Jesus cursed the tree and the tree withered immediately which was witnessed by the disciples. However, Mark says Jesus cursed the tree and only on the following day morning the disciples saw it withered. This is a clear discrepancy and which is why the Bible cannot be from God.*
Response: Again, the discrepancy between Matthew's account and Mark's account exist only in the minds of the skeptic Muslims, but not in the text. Before making a careful study of both accounts let's first see the texts in question in their proper contexts:

"*[18] Now in the morning as He returned into the city, He hungered. [19] And when He saw a fig tree by the wayside, He came to it and found nothing thereon, but leaves only. And He said unto it, "Let no fruit grow on thee henceforward for ever." And immediately the fig tree withered away. [20] And when the disciples saw it, they marveled, saying, "How soon has the fig tree*

withered away!" *²¹ Jesus answered and said unto them, "Verily I say unto you, if ye have faith and doubt not, ye shall not only do this which is done to the fig tree, but also if ye shall say unto this mountain, 'Be thou removed and be thou cast into the sea,' it shall be done. ²² And all things whatsoever ye shall ask in prayer, believing, ye shall receive."* (Matt.21:18-22) KJ21
"¹² And on the morrow, when they had come from Bethany, He was hungry; ¹³ and seeing a fig tree afar off having leaves, He went to see if perhaps He might find any thing thereon. But when He came to it He found nothing but leaves, for the time for figs was not yet. ¹⁴ And Jesus spoke and said unto it, "Let no man eat fruit of thee hereafter for ever." And His disciples heard it.... ²⁰ And in the morning as they passed by, they saw the fig tree dried up from the roots. ²¹ And Peter, calling to remembrance, said unto Him, "Master, behold, the fig tree which Thou cursed is withered away." ²² And Jesus answering, said unto them, "Have faith in God. ²³ For verily I say unto you, that whosoever shall say unto this mountain, 'Be thou removed, and be thou cast into the sea,' and shall not doubt in his heart, but shall believe that those things which he saith shall come to pass, he shall have whatsoever he saith. ²⁴ Therefore I say unto you, what things so ever ye desire when ye pray, believe that ye receive them, and ye shall have them." (Mk.11:12-14…20-24) KJ21

In Matthew we see *"And immediately the fig tree withered away. ²⁰ And when the disciples saw it, they marveled, saying, "How soon has the fig tree withered away!"* (Matt.21:19-20). But in Mark we read, *"And in the morning as they passed by, they saw the fig tree dried up from the roots. ²¹ And Peter, calling to remembrance, said unto Him, "Master, behold, the fig tree which Thou cursed is withered away."* (Mk.11:20-21).

This seems to pose a problem for Muslim friends. However, in reality there exists no problem between these two verses. The following is the explanation of the apparent discrepancy.

As Matthew says 'immediately' the tree withered. But, how soon does the word 'immediately' indicate here? We don't know. It could be in a few seconds or minutes or an hour, still it's immediately for an entire tree to wither.

Another possibility could be that the process of withering had started from the roots up the moment Jesus finished uttering the sentence of cursing the tree and completed after an hour or two. In any case, the tree withered but in all likelihood the disciples could not see it with their naked eyes at that time. However, they heard the curse Jesus uttered and then they all left that place.

The statement *'immediately the tree withered'* was stated only as a matter of fact by the writer of the narration. They all returned the next morning to the same place. By now the process of withering had been completed and was clearly visible to the naked eyes of the disciples. That is why Peter as the representative of the rest spoke to Jesus and remarked that the fig tree got withered because of the curse. With this understanding of the text and context we see that the objection of discrepancy in this regard is only a misunderstood case.

Numerical discrepancies

In my twenty-eight years of born-again Christian life I've personally seen and met hundreds if not thousands of Muslims who became Christians after finding the truth of Jesus Christ during my travels and work in more than a dozen countries. However, a few years ago for the first time in my life along with my wife I had the opportunity to meet and spend a couple of hours with a young Muslim man who had been a Christian prior to becoming a Muslim.

During our friendly chat he told me that one of the reasons why he left Christianity and chose Islam was the discovery he had made about the numerical discrepancies in the Bible with the help of his Muslim friends. We didn't get a chance to discuss with him about it in depth, but only listened to what he had to say about his so-called discovery. Cases like this were rare in the past but are now increasing in number and frequency.

As committed Christians it is appropriate for us to be aware of the so-called discrepancies in the Bible and the proper solutions to them not only for our safety but also to help other Christians who might be on the verge of becoming victims of the lies that are being perpetuated against the Bible. Let's examine some of them now.

Objection # 39: *The Bible contains numerical discrepancies and therefore it is not from God.*

Response: The discrepancies one finds in the Bible come either from translation nuances when the Scriptures were translated from their original languages to other languages or because in some ancient copies some of the letters and words got rubbed off due to repeated use of the manuscript copies over many generations or copyist's mistakes in some but not all of the ancient hand-written manuscripts.

One might find several such instances in different translations in different languages. But the fact is, they get cleared up once we understand how and where they occurred and compare with the other ancient copies extant. Hence this objection is an unscholarly objection to the fact that the Bible is from God.

Objection # 40: *In one passage the Bible states that "Jehoiachin was eighteen years old when he became king" (2 Kings 24:8) while in another it says "Jehoiachin was eight years old when he began to reign" (2 Chronicles 36:9) as given in NASB. The discrepancies in these two accounts of the same incident is a clear proof that the Bible is not from God.*

Response: This discrepancy might have resulted when the single letter for 'ten' in Hebrew language in 2 Chronicles 36:9 had been erased due to repeated usage of the manuscript. The later copyists copied it as it appeared to them rather than verifying it with other copies extant in their time or perhaps they didn't have access to other copies for verification. This natural error got carried over into many Hebrew manuscript copies in the subsequent generations. However, bear in mind that this is not the case with every single manuscript that we have today.

"Jehoiachin was eighteen years old when he became king, and he reigned in Jerusalem three months. His mother's name was Nehushta daughter of Elnathan; she was from Jerusalem." (2 Kings 24:8) NIV

"Jehoiachin was eighteen[a] years old when he became king, and he reigned in Jerusalem three months and ten days. He did evil in the eyes of the LORD." (2 Chronicles 36:9) NIV

NIV Footnote:

    a. 2 Chronicles 36:9 One Hebrew manuscript, some Septuagint manuscripts and Syriac (see also 2 Kings 24:8); most Hebrew manuscripts *eight*

Objection # 41: *In one passage in the Old Testament it says that "David slew of the Syrians the men of seven hundred chariots" (2 Samuel 10:18) while in another passage it is recorded that "David slew of the Syrians the men of seven thousand chariots" (1 Chronicles 19:18). Here too the discrepancy in these two accounts of the same event proves that the Bible is not from God.*

Response: Here the discrepancy arose due to translation nuances. The two verses given below according to the 21st Century King James Version translation show no essential discrepancy between them.

"And the Syrians fled before Israel; and David slew the men of seven hundred chariots of the Syrians and forty thousand horsemen, and smote Shobach the captain of their host, who died there." (2 Samuel 10:18) KJ21

"But the Syrians fled before Israel; and David slew of the Syrians seven thousand men who fought in chariots and forty thousand footmen, and killed Shophach the captain of the host." (1 Chronicles 19:18) KJ21

In 2 Samuel we see, *'David slew the men of seven hundred chariots'*

In 2 Chronicles 19:18 we see, *'David slew of the Syrians seven thousand men who fought in chariots'*

Both do not conflict with each other. The first one tells us the number of chariots i.e.700, that were used in that war by the Syrians. Apparently these chariots might have had several soldiers on each of them and had been used several times over during that war.

The second one tells us the total number of the Syrian soldiers as 7000, who had been killed by David. These seven thousand Syrian soldiers fought with David and his army using those 700 chariots several times during that war. As and when either the weapon-carrying charioteers or the drivers of the chariots were killed during the fighting the same chariots were used again with new replacements.

Objection # 42: *What did the LORD decree 3 years famine (1 Chro.21:11) or 7 years famine (2Sam.24:13)? This discrepancy is a proof for the fact that the Bible is not from God!*

Response: No, it's only a proof that some copies were made with scribal errors. Some Hebrew copies have '7' years of famine that could be scribal errors in some copies; however the Septuagint copies have '3 years of famine' as noted in the NIV Bible.

Objection # 43: *Is it two thousand baths (1Kin.7:26) or three thousand baths (2Chro.4:5)? This discrepancy in the Bible proves it is not from God!*
Response: This discrepancy exists in the mind of the critique due to faulty understanding of the verse, but not in the Bible itself. Let's see the verses and what they imply:
"It was a handbreadth thick, with its brim fashioned like the brim of a cup. Similar in shape to a lily blossom, it could hold 3,000 baths." (2Chro.4:5) ISV
"The reservoir, which held about 2,000 baths, stood about a handbreadth thick, and its rim looked like the brim of a cup or of a lily blossom." (1Kin.7:26) ISV

If we read the above two verses carefully, we understand that the capacity of the reservoir – the subject of the two verses - is 3,000 baths. Nonetheless, it held only 2,000 baths as it was not filled in to its brim during its service for the obvious reason i.e. to avoid spill over!

Objection # 44: *Solomon had **forty thousand** stalls of horses (1 Kings 4:26) in comparison with another which states that the number was **four thousand** (2 Chronicles 9:25). The discrepancy in these two verses also proves that the Bible is not from God.*
Response: Although Hebrew manuscript copies of 1 Kings 4:26 say that Solomon had 'forty thousand' stalls of horses, yet Septuagint (Greek translation of the O.T.) manuscript copies say that Solomon had 'four thousand' stalls of horses. However, in both Hebrew and Septuagint manuscript copies of 2 Chronicles 9:25 we see that Solomon had 'four thousand' stalls of horses. The translation of the above two verses according to the New International Version as given below.

2 Chronicles 9:25 New International Version (NIV):

²⁵ Solomon had four thousand stalls for horses and chariots, and twelve thousand horses,[a] which he kept in the chariot cities and also with him in Jerusalem. (2 Chronicles 9:25) NIV

Footnotes:
   a. 2 Chronicles 9:25 Or *charioteers*

1 Kings 4:26 New International Version (NIV)
²⁶ Solomon had four[a] thousand stalls for chariot horses, and twelve thousand horses.[b]

Footnotes:
   a. 1 Kings 4:26 Some Septuagint manuscripts (see also 2 Chron. 9:25); Hebrew *forty*
   b. 1 Kings 4:26 Or *charioteers*

Question to Muslims

Question: If you think the discrepancies present only in some of the 'copies' of the Holy Bible can make you think that the Holy Bible is not from God, then don't you think that the discrepancies present in the teachings of the Qur'an confirm the fact that the Qur'an is not from the true God?

Example:

"He rules (all) affairs from the heavens to the earth: in the end will (all affairs) go up to Him, on a Day, the space whereof will be (as) <u>a thousand years</u> of your reckoning." (S. 32:5)

"The angels and the spirit ascend unto him in a Day the measure whereof is (as) <u>fifty thousand years</u>." (S. 70:4)

Objection # 45: *The way Jesus' disciples followed him were given in conflicting accounts (Matt.4:12-22 & Jn.1:35-42). Therefore it is not Allah's (God's) word.*

Response: The two narrations of Mathew and John with regard to Jesus' choosing of His disciples are not contradicting, but complementing each other as we can see below. There are three important things to bear in mind while trying to understand from these two narrations. One, these narrations are not meant to be the exhaustive summaries of the events related to Jesus' choosing of His disciples and the way they responded to His call. Second,

Mathew is not necessarily referring to Jesus' first ever meeting with His disciples in his narration. Three, the time between Jesus' temptation and His return to Galilee as Matthew reports (4:12) could be anywhere between several days to several months. With this in mind we can understand that the gist of the two narrations would be as given below:

- Jesus goes up to the Jordan to be baptized by John the Baptist where the latter witnesses the Spirit coming down upon Jesus confirming that He is the Christ.
- Jesus then spends forty days in the desert to be tempted by the Devil.
- After this period Jesus returns to Judea where John the Baptist testifies that he had seen the Spirit descend upon Christ referring to the previous incident.
- It is at this point Jesus meets some of his disciples for the first time. Notice in John's account (1:35-42) it is implied that Jesus had met some of His disciples for the first time.
- Andrew who had been John's disciple of sorts initially met Jesus first along with another disciple of John. After spending just one night where Jesus stayed Andrew brought his own brother Peter and introduced him to Jesus.
- In all likelihood, after meeting with Jesus both Andrew and Peter had returned to their place and work in Galilee.
- Jesus returns with his few other disciples, not necessarily the ten other disciples, to Galilee to attend a wedding.
- Christ and his followers go back to Jerusalem to observe Passover there.
- Having heard that John had been arrested and sensing that the Pharisees were starting to get hostile Jesus returns to Galilee.
- This is where the events narrated by Matthew in chapter 4 from verses 12-22 begin to transpire. At this point Jesus re-gathers some of his followers, who had returned to their previous careers, in order to continue his Galilean ministry.

- Notice in Matthew's account (4:18-22) it is not mentioned directly or indirectly that Jesus met His disciples for the FIRST TIME! This simply means that Jesus had met Peter and his brother Andrew again for the SECOND TIME.

Question # 46: *The Bible says Jesus is coming back soon. It's been more than two thousand years, still Jesus is not back. That means what the Bible says about Jesus' coming back is false and therefore it is not from God.*
Response: This is a hasty conclusion based on a shallow understanding of the Scriptures and God's purposes.

"Above all, you must understand that in the last days scoffers will come, scoffing and following their own evil desires. They will say, 'Where is this 'coming' he promised? Ever since our ancestors died, everything goes on as it has since the beginning of creation." But they deliberately forget that long ago by God's word the heavens came into being and the earth was formed out of water and by water. By these waters also the world of that time was deluged and destroyed. By the same word the present heavens and earth are reserved for fire, being kept for the day of judgment and destruction of the ungodly. But do not forget this one thing, dear friends: With the Lord a day is like a thousand years, and a thousand years are like a day. The Lord is not slow in keeping his promise, as some understand slowness. Instead he is patient with you, not wanting anyone to perish, but everyone to come to repentance." (2 Peter 3:3-9) NIV

Points to understand from the above verses:

a. For God one day is like a thousand years, and a thousand years are like a day. In that sense it's still just 'two days' for God all these two thousand years!
b. God is not slow in keeping His promise of coming back. However, since He doesn't want anyone to perish He is showing more patience towards all people.
c. The word of God prophesied that there would be scoffers in these days who will be asking the questions like this. Since the prophecy is fulfilled, it only confirms that the Holy Bible is God's word.

Objection # 47: *Jesus taught and preached one thing and Paul taught and preached another thing.*

Response: This objection is not based on facts. In the following table we can see the harmony between Jesus' teachings and Paul's teachings:

Jesus taught/preached	Paul taught/preached
But love your enemies, do good to them, and lend to them without expecting to get anything back. Then your reward will be great, and you will be children of the Most High, because he is kind to the ungrateful and wicked. (Luke 6:35)	Do not be overcome by evil, but overcome evil with good. (Romans 12:21)
The high priest said to him, "I charge you under oath by the living God: Tell us if you are the Messiah, the Son of God." "Yes, it is as you say," Jesus replied. (Matthew 26:63-64)	Paul, a servant of Christ Jesus, called to be an apostle and set apart for the gospel of God - the gospel he promised beforehand through his prophets in the Holy Scriptures regarding his Son, who as to his human nature was a descendant of David, and who through the Spirit of holiness was declared with power to be the Son of God by his resurrection from the dead: Jesus Christ our Lord. (Romans 1:1-4)
If you want to enter life, obey the commandments." (Matthew 19:17)	It is not those who hear the law who are righteous in God's sight, but it is those who obey the law who will be declared righteous. (Romans 2:13)
(the disciples asked) "Who then can be saved?" Jesus looked at them and said, "With man this is impossible, but with God all things are possible." (Matthew 19:25-26)	Therefore no one will be declared righteous in his (God's) sight by observing the law; rather, through the law we become conscious of sin. ... for all have sinned and fall short of the glory of God. (Romans 3:20-23)
(Jesus said of himself) The Son of Man did not come to be served, but to serve, and to give his life as a ransom for many. (Matthew 20:28)	In your relationships with one another, have the same mindset as Christ Jesus: Who, being in very nature God, did not consider equality with God something to be used to his own advantage; rather, he made himself nothing by taking the very nature of a servant, being made in human likeness. And being found in appearance as a man, he humbled himself by becoming obedient to death—even death on a cross! (Phil.2:5-8)
Then he took the cup, gave thanks and offered it to them, saying, "Drink from it, all of you. This is my blood of the covenant, which is poured out for many for the	For I received from the Lord what I also passed on to you: The Lord Jesus, on the night he was betrayed, took bread, and when he had given thanks, he broke it and said, "This is my body, which is for you; do this in

forgiveness of sins." (Matthew 26:27-28)	remembrance of me." In the same way, after supper he took the cup, saying, "This cup is the new covenant in my blood; do this, whenever you drink it, in remembrance of me." For whenever you eat this bread and drink this cup, you proclaim the Lord's death until he comes. (1Corinthians 11:23-26) God presented him (Jesus) as a sacrifice of atonement. (Romans 3:25)
Then Jesus came to them and said, "All authority in heaven and on earth has been given to me." (Matthew 28:18)	God raised him (Jesus) from the dead and seated him at his right hand in the heavenly realms, far above all rule and authority, power and dominion, and every title that can be given, not only in the present age but also in the one to come. (Ephesians 1:19-21)
Now this is eternal life: that they know you, the only true God, and Jesus Christ, whom you have sent. (John 17:3)	For there is one God and one mediator between God and mankind, the man Christ Jesus, who gave himself as a ransom for all people. This has now been witnessed to at the proper time. (1Tim.2:5-6)
He told them, "This is what is written: The Messiah will suffer and rise from the dead on the third day, and repentance for the forgiveness of sins will be preached in his name to all nations, beginning at Jerusalem. You are witnesses of these things. (Luke 24:46-47)	For what I received I passed on to you as of first importance: that Christ died for our sins according to the Scriptures, that he was buried, that he was raised on the third day according to the Scriptures, and that he appeared to Cephas, and then to the Twelve. (1Corinthians 15:3-5)

Question # 48: *According to Jesus himself John the Baptist is the greatest of all, not Jesus (Matt.11:7-11)! But why do Christians believe that Jesus is the greatest?*

Answer: In Matthew chapter 11 the Lord Jesus Christ made the remarks referring to John the Baptist:

"Truly I tell you, among those born of women there has not risen anyone greater than John the Baptist; yet whoever is least in the kingdom of heaven is greater than he." (Matt.11:11) NIV

In the above verse the Lord Jesus is not comparing Himself with John the Baptist. This fact becomes apparent when we study the biblical phrase 'born of woman' and how it is used in the Bible. This phrase is used to refer to the people who are mortals and have come into this world through sexual procreation process (Job 14:1, 15:14, 25:4; Matt.11:11; Lk.7:28; 1Cor.11:12). In these places the word 'woman/women' is used in a generic sense.

However, we see a distinction has been maintained when a similar phrase was used in the case of Jesus:

*"But when the set time had fully come, God sent his Son, <u>born of **a** woman</u>, born under the law."* (Gal.4:4) NIV

In the above verse the word 'woman' was not used in a generic sense, but in a specific sense excluding the birth of Jesus from the general births of all the children 'born of woman/women' in the world. Therefore Jesus Christ cannot be grouped together with all the other humans who are 'born of woman/women.'

All human beings are 'born of women' i.e. through sexual procreation process. John is also like one of them for he was also 'born of women' i.e. through the sexual procreation process. John is one of them and he is the greatest of them all. But Jesus Himself is not included in this category for He was not one of them as He was not 'born of women' like everyone else i.e. through sexual procreation process, but was 'born of **a** woman supernaturally.'

If John is compared with the rest of the human beings, who are like him in the way they were born, then John the Baptist is the greatest of all. However, when compared with Jesus, who was not born like the rest of the human beings, John is not greater than Jesus. We can see this truth in John's own words:

"I baptize you with water for repentance. But <u>after me comes one who is more powerful than I, whose sandals I am not worthy to carry.</u> He will baptize you with the Holy Spirit and fire." (Matt.3:11) NIV

"John testified concerning him. He cried out, saying, "<u>This is the one I spoke about when I said, 'He who comes after me has surpassed me because he was before me.</u>'" (Jn.1:15) NIV

"The next day John saw Jesus coming toward him and said, "Look, the Lamb of God, who takes away the sin of the world! <u>This is the one I meant when I said, 'A man who comes after me has surpassed me because he was before me.</u>'" (Jn.1:29-30) NIV

"He must become greater; I must become less. <u>The one who comes from above is above all</u>; the one who is from the earth belongs to the earth, and speaks as one from the earth. <u>The one who comes from heaven is above all.</u>" (Jn.3:30-31) NIV

Objection # 49: *In the O.T. God had cursed the king Jeconiah of Judah and made his descendants unfit for the throne of David (Jer.22:28-30). In the N.T. the genealogy of Jesus in Matthew shows us that Jesus was the descendant of King Jeconiah (Matt.1:11-12). If the O.T. is true then Jesus had already been disqualified to be the King of Jews and has no right to the throne of David.*

Response: Jesus Christ's royal or Davidic lineage comes through Solomon, and through Jeconiah (Matt.1:11). But Jeconiah was cursed by God (Jer.22:28-30) so that his descendants had been barred from sitting on the throne of David. However, the fact is that the curses of God continue only up to the third and the fourth generations (Ex.20:5, 34:7; Num.14:18; Deut.5:9). Since Joseph the foster father of Jesus comes many generations after Jechoniah the curse of Jeconiah was no longer applicable to Joseph and his adopted son Jesus!

Some more contradictions

Question # 50: *The Bible says in one place that Jesus became a cursed one (Gal.3:13), but the same Bible says in another place that he who says Jesus is cursed is not from God's spirit (1Cor.12:3). This is a contradiction and therefore the Bible cannot be from God.*

Response: The following is what the Bible says:
"Christ redeemed us from the curse of the Law, having become a curse (Greek: κατάρα, *katara*) for us—for it is written, "CURSED IS EVERYONE WHO HANGS ON A TREE"—" (Galatians 3:13) NASB
"Therefore I make known to you that no one speaking by the Spirit of God says, "Jesus is accursed" (Greek: ἀνάθεμα, *anathema*); and no one can say, "Jesus is Lord," except by the Holy Spirit." (1 Corinthians 12:3) NASB

Because of sin all humans are sinners and therefore have become cursed of God. Jesus is the only human who lived a perfect and holy life. He never sinned nor acquired God's curse. However, He voluntarily chose to step into our place and receive all the punishment of God's curse that is due to us the sinners in order to redeem us from that predicament. Every person who believes in this God's provision of redemption will be saved.

In short, Jesus was not accursed (*anathema*), but became the object of God's judgment (*katara*) in our place on our behalf.

Objection # 51: *The Bible says in one place that Jesus told his disciples not to go to the gentiles, but in another place we see Jesus saying to his disciples, 'Go to all the nations.' It's a clear contradiction and therefore it's not from God.*

Response: There is time for everything (Eccl.3:1). Initially, Jesus did not allow His disciples to enter into the cities of gentiles. That's only a specific instruction give to the disciples for just one time. However, when the fullness of time came Jesus Himself commissioned His disciples to go to all the nations to preach the gospel and make disciples (Matthew 28:19-20; Mark 16:15-16).

Objection # 52: *According to the Bible Jesus told that he would come back for the second time during the lifetime of his generation (Lk.9:23-36). It did not happen and therefore the Bible is not from God.*

Response: First, let's see what the Bible says about this.

"*²³Then he said to them all: "Whoever wants to be my disciple must deny themselves and take up their cross daily and follow me. ²⁴ For whoever wants to save their life will lose it, but whoever loses their life for me will save it. ²⁵ What good is it for someone to gain the whole world, and yet lose or forfeit their very self? ²⁶ Whoever is ashamed of me and my words, the Son of Man will be ashamed of them when he comes in his glory and in the glory of the Father and of the holy angels.*

²⁷ "Truly I tell you, some who are standing here will not taste death before they see the kingdom of God."

²⁸ <u>About eight days after Jesus said this,</u> he took Peter, John and James with him and went up onto a mountain to pray. ²⁹ As he was praying, the appearance of his face changed, and his clothes became as bright as a flash of lightning. ³⁰ Two men, Moses and Elijah, appeared in glorious splendor, talking with Jesus. ³¹ They spoke about his departure, which he was about to bring to fulfillment at Jerusalem. ³² Peter and his companions were very sleepy, but when they became fully awake, they saw his glory and the two men standing with him. ³³ As the men were leaving Jesus, Peter said to him, "Master, it is good for us to be here. Let us put up three shelters—one for you, one for Moses and one for Elijah." (He did not know what he was saying.)

³⁴ While he was speaking, a cloud appeared and covered them, and they were afraid as they entered the cloud. ³⁵ A voice came from the cloud, saying, "This is my Son, whom I have chosen; listen to him." ³⁶ When the voice had spoken, they found that Jesus was alone. The disciples kept this to themselves and did not tell anyone at that time what they had seen." (Luke 9:23-36) NIV

If we study the whole context we understand that there are two different events Jesus is referring to in verse 26 and 27.

From a careful study we can figure out that the verses 23-26 of chapter 9 form a unit. They are spoken by Jesus in the context of explaining the discipleship and its reward on the last day. It is in this context He is referring, in verse 26, to His second coming on the last day. However, the content of verse 27 is far removed from the previous verse. Here in 27 Jesus spoke of the imminent beginning of His Kingdom that was about to be initiated like a seed or leaven that would grow and spread silently. This verse is the introduction to what had happened in the very next few verses i.e. 28-36.

The words *'About eight days after Jesus said this'* in the beginning of verse 28 are the connecting words to the previous verse i.e. 27. In fact, these words are pointing us to the fulfilment of the event that was spoken of by Jesus when He said, *'Truly I tell you, some who are standing here will not taste death before they see the Son of Man coming in his kingdom.'* (Matthew 16:28) NIV

Here Jesus had predicted a special event that would mark the 'beginning' of Him coming in His kingdom. That's about His glory to be revealed to the disciples and the Father Himself testifying the identity of Jesus to them and commanding them to listen to Him. All these were witnessed by the disciples. They were the people who had seen this before their death as Jesus predicted in verse 27. This is the beginning of the Son of Man coming in his kingdom. This event is not referring to the final day on which the Son of Man would be coming for the second time in His Father's glory with His angels, as described in verse 26, in order to culminate the formation of the Kingdom of God and establish its rule everywhere.

At Jesus' transfiguration event the Kingdom of God had begun. That is why, from hence forth Jesus started to say that the kingdom of God is among you:

"Once, on being asked by the Pharisees when the kingdom of God would come, Jesus replied, "The coming of the kingdom of God is not something that can be observed, nor will people say, 'Here it is,' or 'There it is,' <u>because the kingdom of God is in your midst</u>." (Luke 17:20-21) NIV

But, now the Kingdom of God is spreading and increasing like leaven till the day when Jesus comes for the second time with His Father's glory and with His angels in order to establish His kingdom on earth.

Objection # 53: *According to the Bible in one place John the Baptist was the Elijah to come (Matthew 11:14; 17:10-13) and in another place he was not the Elijah to come (John 1:19-21). This contradiction is a real contradiction and therefore the Bible cannot be from God.*
Response: This so-called contradiction is only an apparent contradiction. If we pay close attention to the texts as well as contexts we can easily see this truth. First let us see the verses in question:

*"For all the Prophets and the Law prophesied until John. And if you are willing to accept it, <u>he is the **Elijah** who was to come</u>. Whoever has ears, let them hear."* (Matt.11:13-15) NIV
*"The disciples asked him, "Why then do the teachers of the law say that Elijah must come first?" Jesus replied, "To be sure, Elijah comes and will restore all things. But I tell you, <u>Elijah has already come</u>, and they did not recognize him, but have done to him everything they wished. In the same way the Son of Man is going to suffer at their hands." Then the <u>disciples understood</u> that he was talking to them about **John the Baptist**."* (Matt.17:10-13) NIV
"Now this was John's testimony when the Jewish leaders in Jerusalem sent priests and Levites to ask him who he was. He did not fail to confess, but confessed freely, "I am not the Messiah."
*They asked him, "Then who are you? <u>Are you **Elijah**?</u>"*

He said, "I am not."
"Are you the Prophet?"
He answered, "No."
Finally they said, "Who are you? Give us an answer to take back to those who sent us. What do you say about yourself?"
John replied in the words of Isaiah the prophet, "I am the voice of one calling in the wilderness, 'Make straight the way for the Lord.'" (Jn.1:19-21) NIV

Let's look into few other verses that help us resolve the apparent confusion:

*"See, I will **send the prophet Elijah** to you before that great and dreadful day of the LORD comes. He will turn the hearts of the parents to their children, and the hearts of the children to their parents; or else I will come and strike the land with total destruction."* (Mal.4:5-6) NIV

*"Then an angel of the Lord appeared to him, standing at the right side of the altar of incense. When Zechariah saw him, he was startled and was gripped with fear. But the angel said to him: "Do not be afraid, Zechariah; your prayer has been heard. Your wife Elizabeth will bear you a son, and you are to call him John. He will be a joy and delight to you, and many will rejoice because of his birth, for he will be great in the sight of the Lord. He is never to take wine or other fermented drink, and he will be filled with the Holy Spirit even before he is born. He will bring back many of the people of Israel to the Lord their God. And he will go on before the Lord, **in the spirit and power of Elijah**, to turn the hearts of the parents to their children and the disobedient to the wisdom of the righteous—to make ready a people prepared for the Lord."* (Lk. 1:11-17) NIV

Now the following points are what we can glean from the above verses. These points shed light on the issue at hand:

a. Jesus testified that John the Baptist was the 'Elijah to come,' but then He adds the phrase, 'whoever has ears, let them hear.' This particular phrase is used by Jesus three times in the gospels and seven times in the Book of Revelation. These contexts show us that it is used by Jesus to underscore the fact that not necessarily all of His audience would understand and accept what He had just said. The main reason for such a possibility is because His words are cryptic to the listeners so that only those who are genuinely open to the truth can understand them.

b. When Jews asked John the Baptist, "Then who are you? Are you Elijah?" He said, "I am not." But had the Jews asked him, "Are you the one the prophet Malachi spoke of as 'Elijah'?" John would have replied affirmatively.

c. In Malachi (4:5-6) it had been prophesied that Elijah would be sent to Israel. But, how was Elijah going to come? Was it in the form of another man or directly descending from heaven or in some other way? In Luke (1:17) the angel Gabriel answers that question by saying, 'in the spirit and power of Elijah.' This seemed a farfetched idea to the Jews whose ears and hearts were closed to God's truth. For this reason Jesus used the phrase, 'whoever has ears, let them hear.'

d. Finally, we can summarize that John the Baptist was not 'Elijah' literally, yet he was indeed 'the Elijah to come' metaphorically since he came in the spirit and power of Elijah.

Objection # 54: *There are many contradictions in the gospels regarding Jesus' death and resurrection accounts. Therefore it is not Allah's (God's) word.*

Response: There are no real contradictions in the Bible. The death and resurrection accounts of Jesus in the four different gospels in the Bible do not conflict, but complement each other. The following summery will demonstrate that to us.

The Lord Jesus Christ was crucified, died and rose again after three days and three nights. However, As opposed to the traditional belief that Jesus was crucified and died on Friday and rose again from the dead on Sunday morning the convincing testimony of the Scriptures as well as the Jewish history point us to a different set of days for these two events. Wednesday being the day of the crucifixion and death of Jesus Christ, Saturday evening becomes His resurrection time. With this in mind the following is the harmony of the death and resurrection accounts of Jesus as presented in the four gospels of the New Testament:

Jesus was arrested after the midnight, tried in the morning just before 6am[1] and crucified at about 9am[2] on Wednesday the 14th Nissan. From 12pm to 3pm there was darkness in the land[3]. He died around 3pm[4] and was buried at about 6pm on the same day[5]. The women followers of Jesus saw all this and went home and rested on the special Sabbath[6].

After the special Sabbath i.e. Thursday [according to the O.T. regular Sabbaths are observed on Saturdays, but seven annual festival days or holy days are also observed as Sabbaths (special) that fall on any day of the week (cf.Ex.12 and Lev.23)], they bought the spices and prepared them (on Friday) and again rested on the regular Sabbath[7] i.e. Saturday. His tomb was sealed on Thursday[8]. He rose again from the dead on Saturday at about 6pm. Sunday morning well before 6am there was an earthquake and an angel of the Lord came to the tomb, removed the stone and sat on it[9]. This made the watchmen fall to the ground as dead persons[10]. After that the angel entered into the tomb and sat at the right side to the place where Jesus' head was lying. Around this time another angel came and joined the first angel and sat at the left side where Jesus' feet were.

After these incidents a group of women followers of Jesus woke up early on Sunday morning before the sunrise and walked up to the tomb to apply the spices they had prepared to His body[11]. They arrived at the tomb at about dawn[12]. However, it was still dark at the tomb due to the trees in the garden[13] and the surrounding hills. Magdalene Mary was one of them[14].

When they approached the tomb while they were still at a distance they saw the stone was removed[15] and the watchmen were lying on the ground[16]. They reasoned that the body of Jesus was stolen. Therefore Mary rushed back leaving the other women in the garden to inform about this to Peter and other disciples[17].

After Mary had left for the city the rest of the women entered the tomb to find out what had happened to the body. Initially, they saw only one angel on the right[18]. Later, both angels appeared to them[19]. The angel on the right spoke to them about Jesus' resurrection and told them to convey the message to the other disciples[20]. They left in haste with joy and shock[21]. They went back to the city but were hesitant to talk to others about it[22].

Around that time Mary Magdalene met the disciples and told them that somebody had stolen Jesus' body[23]. Upon hearing this Peter and John came running to the tomb to find out if what Mary had told them was true[24]. Mary followed them from behind. Peter and John entered the tomb. Both angels became invisible to them! They could see only the clothes, but not Jesus' body. They were perplexed and went back home[25].

Later, Mary Magdalene came to the tomb and entered in it. There she sees the angels for they become visible again. The one on the right side spoke to her[26]. When she looked back she saw Jesus standing, but thought it was the gardener as it was still early in the morning and dark in the shadows of the trees in the garden. But, when Jesus called her 'Mary,' she recognized Him[27]. Jesus spoke to her and sent her to His disciples with a message [28].

After this Jesus appeared to the other women in the city while they were still in a state of shock that caused them to delay meeting the disciples and conveying the message they had received from the angels. They saw the resurrected Jesus and worshiped Him. Jesus spoke to them and sent them to the disciples with a message[29].

Meanwhile, the watchmen woke up and ran into the city and told the Jewish leaders about the incident[30].

By now most of the disciples gathered together to talk about the missing body of Jesus. However, they heard even more surprising news that Jesus rose from the dead and appeared to Mary[31] and the other women for they came to them and related all that had happened to them[32]!

There are no contradictions in the above accounts!

[[1]Jn.18:28, 19:14; [2]Mk.15:25; [3]Mat.27:45, Mk.15:33, Lk.23:44; [4]Mk.15:33-37; [5]Mk.15:42-47; [6]Jn.19:31 cf.Lev.23:32; [7]Lk.23:56; [8]Mat.27:62-66; [9]Mat.28:2; [10]Mat.28:40; [11]Mk.16:1-2, Lk.24:1; [12]Matt.28:1; [13]Jn.20:1; [14]Mat.28:1, Jn.20:1; [15]Mk. 16:4, Lk.24:2, Jn.20:1; [16]Mat.28:5; [17]Jn.20:2; [18]Mk.16:5; [19]Lk.24:4; [20]Mat.28:6-7; [21]Mat.28:8, Mk.16:8; [22]Mk.16:8; [23]Jn.20:2; [24]Jn.20:3; [25]Jn.20:4-10; [26]Jn.20:11-13; [27]Jn.2014-16; [28]Mk.16:9; Jn.20:17; [29]Mat.28:9-10; [30]Mat.28:11-15; [31]Mk.16:11, Lk.24:10, Jn.20:18; [32]Lk.24:9]

Objection # 55: *There are contradictions or errors between the two genealogies of Jesus given in Matthew and Luke. Therefore it is not Allah's (God's) word.*

The Holy Bible: Muslim Objections and Christian Responses

Response: A careful study of the two genealogies given in Matthew and Luke would reveal that they do not contradict with each other at all. In reality, these are two different genealogies of Jesus—one is of his foster father Joseph and the other is of His mother Mary. Let's study the following information from the Bible in the tabular form:

S.N.	Genealogy of Jesus Christ according to Matthew (Matt.1:1-16) (NIV)	Genealogy of Jesus Christ according to Luke (Lk.3:23-38) (NIV)
1.		God created Adam personally and Adam was of God (Adam was considered the *son* of God!)
2.		from Adam came Seth
3.		...Seth...Enosh
4.		...Enosh...Kenan
5.		...Kenan...Mahalalel
6.		...Mahalalel...Jared
7.		...Jared...Enoch
8.		...Enoch...Methuselah
9.		...Methuselah...Lamech
10.		...Lamech...Noah
11.		...Noah...Shem
12.		...Shem...Arphaxad
13.		...Arphaxad...Cainan
14.		...Cainan...Shelah
15.		...Shelah...Eber
16.		...Eber...Peleg
17.		...Peleg...Reu
18.		...Reu...Serug
19.		...Serug...Nahor
20.		...Nahor...Terah
21.		...Terah...Abraham
22.	**Abraham was the father of Isaac**	**...Abraham...Isaac**
23.	Isaac...Jacob	...Isaac...Jacob
24.	Jacob...Judah	...Jacob...Judah
25.	Judah...Perez	...Judah...Perez
26.	Perez...Hezron	...Perez...Hezron
27.	Hezron...Ram	...Hezron...Ram
28.	Ram...Amminadab	...Ram...Amminadab
29.	Amminadab...Nahshon	...Amminadab...Nahshon
30.	Nahshon...Salmon	...Nahshon...Sala
31.	Salmon...Boaz	...Salmon...Boaz
32.	Boaz...Obed	...Boaz...Obed
33.	Obed...Jesse	...Obed...Jesse
34.	Jesse...David	...Jesse...David
35.	**David...Solomon, Nathan**	**...David...Nathan, Solomon and other**

MUSLIM QUESTIONS AND CHRISTIAN ANSWERS | 175

	and other sons	sons
36.	**Solomon**...Rehoboam	...**Nathan**...Mattatha
37.	Rehoboam...Abijah	...Mattatha...Menna
38.	Abijah...Asa	...Menna...Melea
39.	Asa...Jehoshaphat	...Melea...Eliakim
40.	Jehoshaphat...Joram	...Eliakim...Jonam
41.	Joram...Uzziah	...Jonam...Joseph
42.	Uzziah...Jotham	...Joseph...Judah
43.	Jotham...Ahaz	...Judah...Simeon
44.	Ahaz...Hezekiah	...Simeon...Levi
45.	Hezekiah...Manasseh	...Levi...Matthat
46.	Manasseh...Amon	...Matthat...Jorim
47.	Amon...Josiah	...Jorim...Eliezer
48.	Josiah...Jeconiah	...Eliezer...Joshua
49.	Jeconiah...Shealtiel	...Joshua...Er
50.	Shealtiel...Zerubbabel	...Er...Elmadam
51.	Zerubbabel...Abiud	...Elmadam...Cosam
52.	Abiud...Eliakim	...Cosam...Addi
53.	Eliakim...Azor	...Addi...Melchi
54.	Azor...Zadok	...Melchi...Neri
55.	Zadok...Achim	...Neri...Shealtiel
56.	Achim...Eliud	...Shealtiel...Zerubbabel
57.	Eliud...Eleazar	...Zerubbabel...Rhesa
58.	Eleazar...Matthan	...Rhesa...Joanan
59.	Matthan...Jacob	...Joanan...Joda
60.	Jacob...Joseph	...Joda...Josech
61.	Joseph the husband of Mary the mother of Jesus; Joseph the stepfather of Jesus	...Josech...Semein
62.		...Semein...Mattathias
63.		...Mattathias...Maath
64.		...Maath...Naggai
65.		...Naggai...Esli
66.		...Esli...Nahum
67.		...Nahum...Amos
68.		...Amos...Mattathias
69.		...Mattathias...Joseph
70.		...Joseph...Jannai
71.		...Jennai...Melchi
72.		...Melchi...Levi
73.		...Levi...Matthat
74.		...Matthat...Heli
75.		...Heli...Joseph
76.		Joseph was *considered* the father of Jesus

a) The above two genealogies are not exactly the same all along. Both are same only from Abraham to David. Later, both get separated through two sons of David, namely,

Solomon and Nathan. We see many similar names between Solomon and Nathan lineages, but that doesn't mean those names refer to the same individuals.

b) In the Bible the word 'son/sons' can mean…
- a biological son(s); like in the case of Seth 'the son of Adam,' Solomon 'the son of David' etc.
- a descendant(s); like in the case of Jesus 'the son of David,' Israelites are 'the sons of Israel' or 'the children of Abraham,' the Levitical priests were called 'the sons of Levi' etc.
- a special relation; like in the case of Jesus 'the Son of God.'
- a metaphorical son(s); like in the case of a true believer is 'a son of Abraham,' 'child of God' etc.

c) For God's own reasons sometimes some names are left out by the inspired writers in the genealogical narrations, yet we see the phrase 'son of' in those instances, in which case it could mean 'descendant of.'

d) In the above two genealogies Matthew's main focus is to highlight Jesus' Jewishness and His right to the throne of David through His Messiahship. This is why Mathew started the genealogy from Abraham through David, and through David's son Solomon to Joseph, Jesus' stepfather. Luke's account on the other hand is to highlight Jesus' relatedness and relevance to the whole of mankind. That is why Luke starts the genealogy all the way from Adam through Abraham, through David and through David's other son Nathan till Mary's father Heli. This approach reinforces the fact that Jesus' mission was not just for the Jews of his time but for the whole mankind of all times.

Question # 56: *The Bible says in one place that God incited David to take a census of the people and in another place it says Satan incited him to do that. This is a clear contradiction and therefore it is not from God.*
Response: First, let's see what the Bible says:

"Now again the anger of the LORD burned against Israel, and it incited David against them to say, "Go, number Israel and Judah." (2 Samuel 24:1) NASB

"Then Satan stood up against Israel and moved David to number Israel." (1Chronicles 21:1) NASB

God is the sovereign Lord of all. He fulfils His purposes in His creation through angels or humans or nature or even Satan and the other evil spirits. God in His sovereignty allowed David to be incited against Israel. That does not necessarily mean that God did it directly Himself. Since God can use any agent of His choice He chose Satan to do that job. This is not a contradiction at all!

Objection # 57: *The Bible portrays Jesus as calling non-Jews dogs! That is why it is not Allah's (God's) word.*
Response: This is a hasty conclusion based on shallow understanding of the contents and context of the Bible.

"Leaving that place, Jesus withdrew to the region of Tyre and Sidon. A Canaanite woman from that vicinity came to him, crying out, "Lord, Son of David, have mercy on me! My daughter is demon-possessed and suffering terribly." Jesus did not answer a word. So his disciples came to him and urged him, "Send her away, for she keeps crying out after us." He answered, "I was sent only to the lost sheep of Israel." The woman came and knelt before him. "Lord, help me!" she said. He replied, "It is not right to take the children's bread and toss it to the dogs." "Yes it is, Lord," she said. "Even the dogs eat the crumbs that fall from their master's table." Then Jesus said to her, "Woman, you have great faith! Your request is granted." And her daughter was healed at that moment." (Matt.15:21-28) NIV

Before making some notes of the above passage we need to know that the Greek word 'kunarion' (κυνάριον), which means a little dog or puppy, in verses 26 and 27 has been translated as 'dogs' in some translations. This is inaccurate. A grown up dog is called 'kuon' (κύων) in Greek (eg.Phil3:2). And also we need to be aware of the fact that Jesus referred to a proverb of that time in verse 26 in his conversation with the Canaanite woman.

In the above passage of the Bible we need to make the following observations:

a) Jesus was in a foreign land called the region of Tyre and Sidon.

b) There He was requested by a non-Jewish woman to heal her daughter.
c) Initially Jesus did not answer her. It could be that He wanted to test her faith just as He did with many others in the Bible.
d) When disciples urged him to send her away He told them that He was 'sent only to' the lost sheep of Israel. Does this mean that He was not allowed to go to the non-Jewish people to preach and heal them? Not really. Jesus did go to the non-Jewish people and preached gospel as well as healed them (eg. Matt.8:5-13, 28-34, 15:21; Lk.9:52, 17:11-19; Jn.4:5-26). 'Sent only to' does not necessarily limit His overall relevance to other people of all times. Although Jesus was 'sent only to' certain people of His time, yet undoubtedly He was 'meant for all' as the Scriptures testify (Matt.12:18,21; Lk.2:32; Jn.1:29, 12:47). We need to ask ourselves, what for Jesus was 'sent only to' the lost Jews? The answer to this question is Jesus was sent only to the 'lost Jews' in order to be born among them, live among them and fulfill the Father's will among them and be rejected by them as the prophecies had foretold, but NOT just to be a prophet and saviour only to the lost Jews.
e) When the woman made the request He told her a proverb of their time i.e. 'It is not right to take the children's bread and toss it to the dog's children.' By referring to this proverb of their time Jesus is testing the faith as well as humility of the Canaanite woman.
f) Jesus did not call the woman or other non-Jews 'dogs.' Nowhere do we see in the Bible Jesus referring to the Gentiles as, 'You are a dog' or 'all non-Jews are dogs' etc.
g) Finally when the woman demonstrated her faith in Jesus and expressed her humility before Him He did laud her for that and granted her daughter healing.
h) Had Jesus regarded the Gentiles as 'dogs' and was not 'meant' to help them, then He would not have lauded the faith of this Canaanite woman and healed her daughter.

In conclusion, the Bible does not portray Jesus calling non-Jews as dogs.

Objection # 58: *The Bible instructs children to hate their parents (Lk.14:26). That's why it is not Allah's (God's) word.*

Response: This objection is based on wrong understanding and misinterpretation. The Lord Jesus Christ said,

"If anyone comes to me and does not hate father and mother, wife and children, brothers and sisters—yes, even their own life—such a person cannot be my disciple." (Lk.14:26) NIV

The same command was expressed in different wordings:

"Anyone who loves their father or mother more than me is not worthy of me; anyone who loves their son or daughter more than me is not worthy of me." (Matt.10:37) NIV

As a matter of fact, in the above verses Jesus is not instructing *children* to hate their parents! In reality, He is commanding His *disciples* to love Him with the utmost love and devotion. In one occasion He even says, *'all may honor the Son, even as they honor the Father'* (Jn.5:23).

Here Jesus is clearly implying that all should honor Jesus as God! With this understanding if we read the above verses then we will see when the disciples' love for Jesus compared with the love they have for their parents or family members or even their own lives it should appear as if they hate their parents or family members or even their own lives! This expression is one of many literary devices used in the Bible. This is called 'hyperbola.' For illiterates or low-literates this expression may sound bit weird, but for literates and matured readers it is not.

Objection # 59: *According to the Bible a prophet of God cursed innocent little children so that they were torn by bears (2Kin. 2:23-24). Therefore it's not Allah's word (God's word)*
Response: This objection is based on wrong interpretation or misrepresentation of the Bible. Let's see what the Bible says in those verses:

"*Then he went up from there to Bethel; and as he was going up by the way, young lads came out from the city and mocked him and said to him, "Go up, you baldhead; go up, you baldhead!" When he looked behind him and saw them, he cursed them in the name of the LORD. Then two female bears came out of the woods and tore up forty-two lads of their number.*" (2 Kin.2:23-24) NASB

Few observations of the verses:

a) The Hebrew phrase '*ne arim qetanim*' is translated as 'young lads.'
b) Even King Solomon calls himself '*ne arim qetanim*' when he sat on his father David's throne (1 Kin.3:7). At that time Solomon was in his late teens.
c) The 'young lads' who mocked the prophet were not innocent little children, but they were a band of rowdy teenagers.
d) These rowdy teenagers were insulting Elisha by calling him 'baldhead.' This also gives us a window into their psyche and nature. In those days in that culture respecting elders and godly people was of utmost important. The behavior and language of these teenagers at this point demonstrating to us their long list of uncontrolled behavior and rowdism that might have gone out of limits.
e) And they were also challenging him to 'go up,' apparently referring to the prophet Elijah's ascension. Their challenge might be the result of their disbelief either in the report of Elijah's ascension or the appointment of Elisha to be a prophet in Elijah's place. Thus they incurred the wrath of the prophet who was anointed by God.
f) The prophet's curse on the teenagers is justified in the light of their current behavior as well as past actions that were completely open before the God of the prophet.

In conclusion, according to the Bible the prophet did not curse some 'innocent children,' but rowdy teenagers.

Question to Muslims

Question: When a prophet of God cursed some rowdy teenagers for their wicked behavior Muslim think it's cruel. What would Muslims say about a

> servant of Allah himself killing an innocent child according to the Qur'an?
>
> *"Then found they one of Our slaves, unto whom We had given mercy from Us, and had taught him knowledge from Our presence...So they twain journeyed on till, when they met a lad, he slew him. (Moses) said: What! Hast thou slain an innocent soul who hath slain no man? Verily thou hast done a horrid thing... And as for the lad, his parents were believers and we feared lest he should oppress them by rebellion and disbelief."* (S. 18:65...74...80)

Objection # 60: *The Bible's teachings such as turn the other cheek to him who slaps you on one cheek (Matt.5:39) and doctrines such as 'Trinity' do not make sense. Therefore it is not Allah's (God's) word.*

Response: This objection reflects ones intellectual weakness. The teachings of the Bible and the doctrines it espouses are the best and highest dictums from God. Some of them may not make sense for everyone, but that doesn't mean they are wrong or bad. Although some of them may not make immediate sense, yet later they do make sense as one grows in the knowledge of God. As far as the doctrine of 'Trinity' is concerned, since it is about God's nature no human being can fully explain it or any human mind can fully comprehend it. That's the greatness of God.

Likewise, there are many teachings and doctrines even in the Qur'an that do not make sense to non-Muslims. Do Muslims accept it as a proof for the falsity of the Qur'an?

Question # 61: *If the Bible is God's word, can any Christian prove what it says in Mark 16:15-18 is true by drinking poison and experiencing no harm?*

Answer: First let us see what Jesus actually said and the context of it.

"And He said to them, "Go into all the world and preach the gospel to all creation. He who has believed and has been baptized shall be saved; but he who has disbelieved shall be condemned. These signs will accompany those who have believed: in My name they will cast out demons, they will speak with new tongues; they will pick up serpents, and if they drink any deadly poison, it will not hurt them; they will lay hands on the sick, and they will recover." (Mk.16:15-18) NASB

Well, the Bible is truly God's word. There are two things to bear in mind when one makes a challenge like the above.

a) The teachings of the Bible should be understood in their relevant literal, cultural and contextual senses. Some instructions are literal and some are metaphorical. Some are applicable only in some cultures and some are for all cultures. Some are for particular contexts and some are for all occasions. Hence, one should be able to discern the difference and understand the intended meaning.
b) The Bible contains instructions as well as promises. One should be able to distinguish one from the other. The instructions of God in the Holy Bile should be obeyed and followed. Whereas the promises of God in the Bible have to be experienced in one's spiritual growth and walk. The promises of God are given not to test God, but to claim and experience them by faith.

With the above in mind, we can see the signs that would accompany those who believe, as given in Mark 16:16-18, are promises of Jesus to the believers, but not instructions for the believers to perform. Particularly in the verse 18 Jesus said, "...*if they drink any deadly poison, it will not hurt them.*" Here Jesus is not telling the believers to go and drink deadly poison!

An example:

Luke 4:9-12
And he (Satan) led Him (Jesus) to Jerusalem and had Him stand on the pinnacle of the temple, and said to Him:
SATAN: "If you are the Son of God, throw Yourself down from here; for it is written (in the Holy Bible), '*He will give His angels charge concerning you to guard you,*' and, '*On their hands they will bear you up, lest you strike your foot against a stone.*'" (cf.Ps.91:11-12)
JESUS: It is said (in the Holy Bible), '*You shall not put the LORD your God to the test.*' (cf.Deut.6:16)

In the above temptation dialogue Satan challenged Jesus with a similar question. But Jesus did not jump off the pinnacle of the temple as the devil tempted Him although it is written that God would put His angels to protect those who trust in God. For Jesus to jump based on the promise in Ps.91:11-12 is to test God, which is forbidden in the Bible.

Our daughter gave her life to Christ and became a child of God when she was six years old. But after turning seven one day while playing in our bedroom she accidentally fell from the window on the fourth floor where we used to live. In that fall she sustained neither a fracture nor an injury! It was nothing short of a miracle even as the doctors who examined her admitted it. Obviously, she was protected by God's angels according to His promise (Ps.91:11-12).

Bear in mind that she did not try to test God in this incident, but accidentally fell from the window. God had proved His promise in her case for the Bible is truly God's word.

Objection # 62: *The Bible portrays Jesus as a disrespectful son towards his mother (Jn.2:4). Therefore it cannot be God's word.*
Response: This objection fails to take into consideration Jesus' identity and His relation to Mary at that point as well as the meaning of the term 'woman' two thousand years ago.

a. Even at the age of twelve Jesus saw Himself as the Son of God (Luke 2:41-51).
b. By the time Jesus was attending the marriage ceremony in Cana He was fully grown up and had already been anointed for His mission in this world.
c. Although Jesus humbled Himself to the point of becoming a child of Mary for a limited and temporal period, yet He is the Creator of all including Mary (Jn.1:1-2; Col.1:16). He is also the Lord of all including Mary. He is the Lord of Mary's relative Elizabeth an old lady (Lk.1:43). He is the Lord of even David the great great great grandfather of both Mary and Joseph (Matt.22:41-45; Acts 2:34, 10:36 cf.Ps.110:1). In the light of these facts it is not unreasonable for Jesus not to call Mary mother!
d. Over several generations words and meanings in languages change. The term 'woman' used to address a female today sounds disrespectful or derogatory, but two thousand years

ago when Jesus used the term 'woman' to address Mary (Jn.2:4) it did not have the same disrespectful or derogatory connotation to it. A better translation of the term today might be a polite 'madam.'

In summary, the objection is based on half-knowledge, and therefore without any substance.

Objection # 63: *The Bible employs questionable language such as fox, dogs and swine to refer to people (Matthew 7:6, 15:26; Lk.13:32; Philippians 3:2). That is why it is not from Allah (God).*

Response: God in the Bible employed 'figure of speech' in which He used animals such as fox, dog and swine for a simile to describe the nature of the wicked people. It would be presumptuous to object to the use of literary techniques including the 'figure of speech' by the Creator!

This Muslim objection is both irrational and hypocritical. God being the Creator and sovereign of all has the authority and freedom to allow His prophets or Apostles to employ 'figure of speech' in describing certain wicked people due to their sinful nature that is akin to some of the animals' nature in a metaphorical sense.

Questions to Muslims

Question#1: If using animals in a metaphorical sense to refer to certain evil people is unworthy of God and unfit for God's word, then why does the Qur'an commit this mistake?

Examples:

"And had We willed We could have raised him by their means, but he clung to the earth and followed his own lust. Therefor his likeness is as the likeness of <u>a dog</u>: if thou attackest him he panteth with his tongue out, and if thou leavest him he panteth with his tongue out. Such is the likeness of the people who deny Our revelations. Narrate unto them the history (of the men of old), that haply they may take thought." (S. 7:176)

"For the <u>worst of beasts</u> in the sight of God are those who reject Him: They will not believe." (S. 8:55)

"The likeness of those who are entrusted with the Law of Moses, yet apply it not, is as the likeness of the <u>ass</u> carrying books. Wretched is the likeness of folk who deny the revelations of Allah. And Allah guideth not wrongdoing folk." (S. 62:5)

Question#2: If just using animals in a metaphorical sense to refer to certain evil people is unworthy of God and unfit for God's word, then why does the Qur'an even goes so far to blame Allah that he not only used animals for metaphorical purposes to refer to people but turned people into actual apes and pigs?

Example:

"Say: "Shall I point out to you something much worse than this, (as judged) by the treatment it received from God? those who incurred the curse of God and His wrath, those of whom some He transformed into <u>apes and swine</u>, those who worshipped evil; - these are (many times) worse in rank, and far more astray from the even path!" (S. 5:60)

Objection # 64: *In the book of Psalms there are many curses by David against his enemies. How can this be from God? Is it not contradictory to what Jesus preached?*

Answer: All the curses that David as a king and prophet hurled against his enemies under God's inspiration in the book of Psalms demonstrate to us that they are legitimate curses uttered by David for he suffered greatly through the actions of his enemies. That's what his enemies deserved and that's the natural standard in dealing with enemies. However, the best standard, as the Lord Jesus showed us, is the ultimate standard. According to this standard we are not to curse our enemies, but to bless them. This is why the best model for all humanity is neither Adam nor Abraham nor Moses nor even David. It's the Lord Jesus Christ!

Question to Muslims

Question: Even in the Qur'an there are curses against enemies, which is normal and understandable. But if the Qur'an is truly from God why doesn't the Qur'an teach God's standard by saying 'love your enemies and pray for those who persecute you' as in the Injeel (Matt.5:44)?

Objection # 65: *The genealogies of Jesus contain the sinful people like Tamar Judah's daughter-in-law (Matt.1:3), Rahab the prostitute (Matt.1:5). This makes the birth of Jesus Christ contaminated and shameful. This is why the Bible is not God's word.*

Response: Not only Tamar and Rahab are sinful persons in Jesus' genealogies, but everyone else in those genealogies is a sinner. In reality, all humans are sinners (1King.8:46; 2Chr.6:36; Ps.143:2; Rom.3:10, 23). There is none who is without sin except Jesus Christ.

The very purpose of Jesus Christ coming into this world is to provide help to sinful people. Having 'sinful' people in the genealogies of Jesus doesn't make the genealogies unholy or not inspired! It is not the mention of the sinful people in the genealogies that affects Jesus, rather it is the other way round. In reality, the very fact that those sinners found place in the genealogies of Jesus affects them positively.

Question to Muslims

Question: If you think the 'sinful' people in the genealogies of Jesus Christ disqualify him as the prophet of God or the very mention of them in the Bible makes it non-divine, then the long list of the sinful people who were idolaters in the family line of the Islamic prophet Muhammad and the mention of the sinful persons such as Pharaoh and Abu Lahab in the Qur'an (S. 2:49; 111:1) should also disqualify Muhammad as a prophet and the Qur'an as divine. Do you agree?

Question # 66: *Jesus Christ was born without a father. How can he who had no father have a genealogy at all? Why did Christians give him the genealogies?*

Answer: Genealogies in the Bible are not given by Jews or Christians. They are given by God through inspiration. They are there in the Bible according to God's plan and purpose.

Although Jesus had no biological father, He had a foster father called Joseph. According to the Biblical culture, like the other civilized cultures of the world today, children received through adoption have equal rights as those of biological children. Only barbaric or uncivilized cultures that are morally bankrupt have other than this attitude toward the adopted children. Jesus as a child adopted by Joseph has been legally and morally included in Joseph's genealogy.

Genealogies in the Scriptures were of utmost importance for the identification of the 'Promised Messiah'—the eternal King, the perpetual Priest and the perfect Prophet. These genealogies provide the *acid test* for those who were waiting eagerly, as the Jewish Scriptures indicate, to identify the true Promised Messiah. They also expose the emptiness of the claims of all the counterfeit promised messiahs who have made claims throughout history, even to this day.

Muslim accusation # 67: *The Bible uses sexual perversion in its descriptions. Therefore it is not Allah's (God's) word.*
Response: The Bible exposes human wickedness and man's sinful nature. It is a spiritual mirror that shows how humans once were and what they have become now. In order to do this it employs 'figures of speech,' 'metaphors' etc. One can see oneself in this mirror and respond appropriately. On the other hand, it also provides the ideals for human sexuality and the male-female relationship within God-approved boundaries.

Objection # 68: *The Bible contains obscene descriptions like in the book of Ezekiel (Ezekiel 23:1-49). Therefore it is not from Allah (God).*
Response: The whole Ezekiel 23 chapter is a 'figure of speech' that employs several metaphors. In the beginning, in verse 4 we see:

"The older was named Oholah, and her sister was Oholibah. They were mine and gave birth to sons and daughters. <u>Oholah is Samaria</u>, and <u>Oholibah is Jerusalem</u>." (Eze.23:4) NIV

The above Scripture makes it abundantly clear that the so-called lewd women, Oholah and Oholibah, were not two literal female human beings. They are two cities—Samaria and Jerusalem. God through Ezekiel is describing the decay of moral values and the rebellion of people against God in these cities in the form of metaphors. It is a scorching rebuke from God to the communities living in these two cities.

The Holy Bible: Muslim Objections and Christian Responses

Objection # 69: *The Bible contains pornographic descriptions and therefore it cannot be from Allah (God)! (Proverbs 5:15-21)*
Response: Here the word of God is instructing young husbands not to be unfaithful to their wives by going to harlots for sexual pleasures. In these instructions God who made the whole of creation including human bodies mentioned female organs.

When a doctor or counselor uses the same language in his instructions we don't see any porn there. How, then, can the Creator's description of the female body be a pornographic description?

Question to Muslims

Question: If you think the mentioning of 'breasts' in the Holy Bible is not worthy of God's word, then by the same standard do you agree even the Qur'an is also not worthy of being Allah's word since it too uses similar language?

"*And Mary, daughter of Imran, who guarded farjahaa* (Arabic: فرْجَهَا=her female sexual organ. This actual meaning is usually avoided in the translations of the Qur'an in other languages. Although there are other words for chastity and virginity in Arabic language the Qur'an uses this explicitly sexual word several times.), *and we breathed **therein** of our spirit and she verified the words of her Lord and His books, and was of the devout.*" (S 66:12)

Objection # 70: *The Bible contains explicit sexual content and therefore it is not from Allah (God). (Songs of Solomon 1:4,13, 4:5,16, 7:3,7-9, 8:8,10)*
Response: As to its literary genre, the Song of Solomon is obviously a poem of love. Song of Solomon describes a conjugal love between a bride and bridegroom. There is no basis for the objection to its divine inspiration for the conjugal love between a bride and bridegroom is a divinely sanctioned relation and that is what is being promoted in it. Furthermore, the kind of language it employs is certainly not outlawed for the Creator to use in His word.

> **Question to Muslims**
>
> **Question:** If you think the presence of the descriptive language about the female organs makes the Holy Bible unworthy of being God's word, then please first let us know what is the acceptable standard for Allah's book to contain and who gives that and where did you find it?

Once I had a dialogue with a Muslim about the explicit language employed in the Bible. Here is the gist of it:

Ahmed: Hi Abdul, how can you call the Bible God's word seeing that it contains such an explicit language that you cannot even allow your own children to read it. For example, please read Ezekiel chapters 16 and 23. That's graphic and repulsive. How can it be from the true God?
Abdul: Ahmed, I see your point. But you failed to see the point of the Holy Bible. In the first place, the so-called explicit language is not intended for children. Apart from that you should also realize as indicated in verse 4 of the chapter 23 that it is not literal but metaphorical. In this chapter of Ezekiel a 'figure of speech' literary technique was used by the Almighty to describe the vulgarity of the sinful behavior of the Jews in Ezekiel's time.
Ahmed: But how can God use such a vulgar language?
Abdul: Well, tell me please, according to your own wisdom can a doctor make references to human private parts in his talk without sounding vulgar? In the same way, can a science teacher talk about human body parts including sexual organs to school children without being accused of using explicit language?
Ahmed: Yes, of course! I don't see any problem there.
Abdul: Well, not only you, no normal person should have any problem there. If you think mere humans such as a doctor and a teacher have the right to use such language how can you suppose that you have the right to tell the Creator of all including human body parts that He has no right to make references to human private parts in His language? What kind of Allah you believe in?
Ahmed: Ok, ok! I see your point.

Accusation # 71: *The Bible promotes incest. Therefore it is not Allah's (God's) word.*
Response: Nothing could be further from the truth! On the contrary, the Bible prohibits incest in detailed statutory instructions.

The Bible condemns incest in Lev.18:6-18. The relationships that God clearly forbade are between a child and a parent, a step-child and a step-parent, a grandchild and a grandparent, a child and a brother or sister of a parent (i.e., an aunt or uncle), siblings, and half-siblings.

Objection # 72: *The Bible promotes incest in the case of Lot and his daughters (Gen.19:30-36) and Judah and Tamar (Gen.38:1-26) and Amnon and Tamar (2Sam.13:1-21). Therefore it is not Allah's (God's) word.*

Response: In our modern days incest is defined as "The crime of sexual intercourse or cohabitation between a man and woman who are related to each other within the degrees wherein marriage is prohibited by law."

3500 years ago, incest was defined and forbidden in the Bible. In fact, various punishments have been specified in the Law of Moses (the Old Testament) for those who get involved in different incestuous relations. The following Bible passage demonstrates that to us:

"If a man has sexual relations with his father's wife, he has dishonored his father. Both the man and the woman are to be put to death; their blood will be on their own heads.

"If a man has sexual relations with his daughter-in-law, both of them are to be put to death. What they have done is a perversion; their blood will be on their own heads.

"If a man has sexual relations with a man as one does with a woman, both of them have done what is detestable. They are to be put to death; their blood will be on their own heads.

"If a man marries both a woman and her mother, it is wicked. Both he and they must be burned in the fire, so that no wickedness will be among you.

"If a man has sexual relations with an animal, he is to be put to death, and you must kill the animal.

"If a woman approaches an animal to have sexual relations with it, kill both the woman and the animal. They are to be put to death; their blood will be on their own heads.

"If a man marries his sister, the daughter of either his father or his mother, and they have sexual relations, it is a disgrace. They are to be publicly removed from their people. He has dishonored his sister and will be held responsible.

"If a man has sexual relations with a woman during her monthly period, he has exposed the source of her flow, and she has also uncovered it. Both of them are to be cut off from their people.

"Do not have sexual relations with the sister of either your mother or your father, for that would dishonor a close relative; both of you would be held responsible.

"If a man has sexual relations with his aunt, he has dishonored his uncle. They will be held responsible; they will die childless.

"If a man marries his brother's wife, it is an act of impurity; he has dishonored his brother. They will be childless." (Leviticus 20:11-20) NIV

However, the Bible also relates the incestuous relations and marriages that did take place in the past. But that doesn't mean the Bible is promoting or sanctioning incest. Bear in mind, not necessarily everything recorded in the Bible is its prescription to us. Most of the incestuous incidents took place prior to the code of marriage relationships given through Moses around 1400 B.C.

The following are some of the 'incestuous' incidents recorded in the Bible. Let's study when and why they occurred:

- *Cain apparently married his own sister* (Gen.4:17).
  All the children of Adam and Eve had committed this. During their time it was neither prohibited nor abhorred nor was avoidable.
- *Daughters of Lot had sexual relations with their father* (Gen.19:30-36).
  At the time of this incident such relations were not explicitly prohibited, but obviously abhorred through the law of conscience (Rom.2:14-15). From the context it is evident that even the daughters of Lot were ashamed of this relation which is why they made their father drunk. Lot was obviously not a willing and conscious partner in this abhorrent act. The reason why the Bible reports this incident is that it highlights in this episode how the way Lot chose the option to go away from

the oversight of a godly man (Abraham) based on the appeal of the physical sight that actually led him to live in a morally decadent society under whose influence he ultimately had his own family met with disaster, physical as well as moral. It also highlights the manifestation of human depravity and evil intent in the absence of societal oversight and accountability.

- *Abraham married his half-sister Sarah* (Gen.20:12).
  This took place 700 years before the marriage between a man and his half-sister was ultimately prohibited.
- *Reuben had sexual relation with his father's concubine* (Gen.35:22).
  This is a shameful act according to the universal moral principles. Reuben was condemned and penalized for committing it (Gen.49:22). This shows us how the fallen nature that enables mankind to commit sin was present even among the children of Jacob whom God had chosen for a divine purpose.
- *Judah had sexual relations with his former 'daughter-in-law'* (Gen.38:1-26).
  This incident had occurred before the code of marriage relations was given. Besides, since Tamar's husband had died and she was denied her rightful marriage to the other son of Judah according to the social norms of that time she was morally not bound by the 'daughter-in-law' relationship to Judah (cf.Rom.7:2-3). This is why even Judah pronounces, *"She is more righteous than I, since I wouldn't give her to my son Shelah."*
- *Moses' father Amram married his aunt Jochebed* (Ex.6:20)
  This also had happened before the marriage relation between a man and his aunt was prohibited.
- *Amnon David's son raped his half-sister Tamar* (2Sam.13:1-21).
  This was clearly a sin committed by Amnon against his half-sister and his father and God. This is recorded like many other incidents in the Bible to disclose human wickedness, especially in the absence of proper parental discipline, even in the family of a godly man, and how it leads to moral decadence and enmity among family members.
- *Absalom David's son raped his father's concubines* (2 Sam. 16:20-22).

This is a shocking sin committed by Absalom against his father's concubines and against his father and against God in clear violation of God's law given through Moses. This he did after leading a coup against his father David and became King in his place. As a result of this and many other wicked things he had committed he met with an ignominious death (2 Sam.18:9-15). Again, this incident demonstrates to us how the sin of adultery committed by David with his neighbor's wife (2 Sam.11:1-27) had finally brought punishment back upon himself as God had pronounced through prophet Nathan (2 Sam.12:11-12). Even David the man after God's own heart was not immune to the dangers of sin in the form of unbridled passions and the divine justice that it would ultimately bring.

Questions to Muslims

Question#1: The Holy Bible mentions certain incestuous relationships both before and after the law was given in order to expose the fallen human nature. However, Muslims think this would disqualify the Holy Bible as God's word. To such Muslims here is a question: Could you tell us why did the Quran approve incestuous relationship in the case of Muhammad's marriage with Zaynab the wife of Muhammad's adopted son as given in the Quran (S.33:37-38)?

Question#2: Interestingly, the above incestuous incident in the Quran is followed by the complete abolition of adoption in Islam through another 'revelation' Muhammad gave in the Quran (S.33:4-5). Adopting orphans as one's own sons and daughters is one of the noblest actions among people of all cultures, religions and times except in some uncivilized and barbaric groups. Is this not a clear proof that Muhammad came up with self-serving revelations through which he tried to justify his own actions and desires?

Question#3: The Holy Bible clearly forbids both homosexuality and bestiality (Exodus 22:19; Leviticus 18:23, 20:13, 15-16; Deuteronomy 27:21; Rom.1:26-27; 1Corinthians 6:9-10), but Quran doesn't. Why does the Quran fail to forbid both homosexuality and bestiality through clear commands?

Objection # 73: *There are words of humans and words of angels and words of animals and even the words of Satan in the Bible which make it not the word of God/Allah.*

Response: This objection is based on pure ignorance as well as hypocrisy. The Bible contains direct speech, indirect speech and reported speech. All these were recorded under divine inspiration.

Because of divine inspiration in its recording the Bible is called God's word, not because every bit of its contents are the actual words spoken by God Himself.

Question to Muslims

Question: If you think the presence of the reported words of ordinary people or angels or devils can disqualify the Holy Bible being God's word, then the same should be done to the Qur'an as well. Since the Qur'an contains the words of ordinary people, angels and Satan (S. 1:1-7; 3:36, 42-43; 4:118-119) do you agree that the Qur'an is also not from Allah?

Objection # 74: *Paul could not give clear-cut instructions, but some suggestions and opinions in the Bible (1Cor.7:25). Therefore it is not from God!*

Response: Here is the verse in question:

"*Now concerning virgins I have no command of the Lord, but <u>I give an opinion</u> as one who by the mercy of the Lord is trustworthy.*" (1Cor.7:25) NASB

In the above verse Paul is giving his personal 'opinion' or 'suggestion' under divine inspiration. In fact, the Bible as well as Qur'an contains opinions of people. However, such opinions need to be understood as reported speech. Like the Qur'an even the Bible contains the reported speeches of ordinary people, prophets, angels and even devils. All such reported words are recorded under inspiration that is why they are part of God's word. One must regard opinions in the Bible either binding or non-binding depending on the contexts. In the above verse the personal opinion of Paul is not to be taken as Lord's command, but only as a wise brotherly advice. In the light of this explanation the above objection to the Bible doesn't hold any water!

Question to Muslims

"*And if ye fear that ye will not deal fairly by the orphans, <u>marry of the women, who seem good to you, two or three or four; and if ye fear that ye cannot do justice (to so many) then one (only) or (the captives) that your right hands possess</u>. Thus it is more likely that ye will not do injustice. And give unto the women (whom ye marry) free gift of their marriage portions; <u>but if they of their own accord remit unto you a part thereof, then ye are welcome to absorb it (in your wealth)</u>.*" (S. 4:3-4)

Question: In the above Qur'anic verse instead of a clear-cut instruction a suggestion or opinion has been expressed. For example, it is not binding on all Muslims that they should marry four wives. However, if a Muslim wants to marry four wives then he should consider the conditions expressed in these verses and decide. Since you think Paul's failure to give clear-cut instructions make it not inspired, do you believe the same with the above verse in the Qur'an?

Objection # 75: *The Gospel of Barnabas is the real 'gospel' or the Injeel, but not the New Testament.*
Response: This is another BIG lie against God's word, the Bible. The Gospel of Barnabas is not the true gospel at all. Even Muslims should reject it for the following reasons:

a) The epistle of Barnabas is a genuine ancient Christian historical book, but the Gospel of Barnabas is a 14th century forgery. These are two different books.
b) The oldest manuscript copies of the Gospel of Barnabas are from 15th century. They were written in Italian and Spanish. Neither in Greek nor Hebrew!
c) The Gospel of Barnabas on Jesus' title:
The gospel of Barnabas initially says: "*God has during these past days visited us by his prophet Jesus <u>Christ</u>*" (p.2). But later we see in it: "*Jesus confessed and said the truth, "<u>I am not the Messiah</u>"* (Chap. 42).
This way the Gospel of Barnabas contradicts its own statement about Jesus i.e. Christ (Messiah), and it also contradicts what the Qur'an says about Jesus: *(And remember) when the angels said: O Mary! Lo! Allah giveth thee glad tidings of a word from him, whose name is <u>the Messiah</u>, Jesus, son of*

Mary, illustrious in the world and the Hereafter, and one of those brought near (unto Allah). (S. 3:45)

d) The Gospel of Barnabas on Jesus' birth:
It says: *The virgin was surrounded by a light exceeding bright, and brought forth her son <u>without pain</u>* (Chap. 3)
This contradicts the Qur'an: *So she conceived him, and she retired with him to a remote place. And <u>the pains of childbirth</u> drove her to the trunk of a palm-tree: <u>She cried (in her anguish)</u>: "Ah! would that I had died before this! would that I had been a thing forgotten and out of sight!* (S. 19:22-23)

e) The Gospel of Barnabas on heavens:
It says: *Verily I say unto thee that <u>the heavens are nine</u>, among which are set the planets, that are distant one from another five hundred years journey for a man* (Chap. 178).
This contradicts what the Qur'an says about the heavens: *<u>The seven heavens</u> and the earth, and all beings therein, declare His glory: there is not a thing but celebrates His praise; And yet ye understand not how they declare His glory! Verily He is Oft-Forbear, Most Forgiving!* (S. 17:44)

If Muslims accept the Gospel of Barnabas as God's word then they should throw their Qur'an because the Gospel of Barnabas contradicts the Qur'anic teachings too! For the above reasons quite a number of Muslim scholars have already rejected the Gospel of Barnabas as the true Gospel Qur'an refers to.

A dialogue

Over the years, again and again I heard Muslims venting their hatred against the Apostle Paul. This is not because they read and found wanting the Scriptures given through Paul, but because they hear so much negative teachings given to them by Muslim apologists about Paul and what he taught. Below, I give a typical dialogue between a Muslim and me:

Muslim: Why do you believe and follow Paul's words?
Abdul: What do you mean by that?
Muslim: Well, the Bible is written by Paul, at least most of the New Testament, right? If you follow the Bible, I mean the New Testament, then

you are actually following Paul but not Jesus.
Abdul: Oh, now I see it. I understand your point. But please tell me first, why do you believe Muhammad's words, I mean the Qur'an, and follow him?
Muslim: Oh no! The Qur'an is not Muhammad's (PBUH) words. They are Allah's words but given through prophet Muhammad.
Abdul: Well, that's what you believe about the Qur'an, right? In the same way, I believe that the Holy Bible is God's word given to us through Paul, Matthew, Mark, Luke John etc. What's your problem?
Muslim: But in the Qur'an Allah says, they are Allah's words.
Abdul: Ok, but that's what Muhammad said! The problem with this is one man by the name Muhammad gave some words and said these are from Allah and those are the words that say Muhammad is Allah's prophet. No other prophet or apostle or a divinely inspired person confirmed it.
Muslim: Allah chose Muhammad (PBUH) to be his prophet and that's why Allah's word the Qur'an was given through prophet Muhammad. What's the problem with that?
Abdul: What's the problem…! Will you accept if someone comes and gives a book saying that it is from Allah and in that book it is written that the person who gave the book is a prophet from Allah?
Muslim: No way. Moreover, how can it be? He cannot be a prophet, but a liar.
Abdul: That's the problem we have with Muhammad's claim. Muhammad himself gave a book and told that the book was from Allah. It is written in that book that Muhammad is a prophet from Allah. This is a circular claim. In other words, Muhammad's prophethood is claimed as well as confirmed by Muhammad himself!
Muslim: So…? What else needs to be done?
Abdul: If a special prophet was sent from God to mankind or God sent His word through a special prophet then that would be confirmed by other prophets of God. For example, Moses was a special prophet who brought God's word the Torah to us. This is confirmed by other prophets of God such as Samuel, David, Isaiah, Daniel, Jesus etc. In the same way, Jesus Christ was a special prophet who made a new covenant between mankind and God. He is the final Prince, Priest and Prophet from God. He was also confirmed by the previous prophets and later apostles. To believe that Muhammad was a prophet from Allah simply because Muhammad himself claimed that he was a prophet from Allah is not a sound and logical belief.
Muslim: How about Paul? How can you believe that his words are from God? You did not have any proof that he is a prophet or apostle apart from himself?
Abdul: Sorry, my friend, you are totally wrong! Paul had been a murderer and a religious fanatic before becoming a Christian. But when he met God's power in a vision he became a new person and a true Christian. After that

The Holy Bible: Muslim Objections and Christian Responses

Paul renounced murdering others and became a preacher of love and forgiveness. He was even martyred for this change in his life and the message he preached. God chose him to be God's Apostle and gave us His word through Paul. We don't say Paul was an Apostle of God just because Paul himself claimed it. Other Apostles confirmed it. His changed life authenticated it. His miracles demonstrated it. Do you have anything genuinely similar to that for Muhammad's prophethood, my friend?
Muslim:……..!

Abdul: Interestingly, in the case of the Apostle Paul, we see a person being transformed from a life of killing and hating others to a life of loving and forgiving even enemies and preaching peace to all. This can happen only by the power of God. If a person had a normal life before a so-called supernatural encounter and after the encounter he becomes a man who preaches violence and involves in killing others that itself is a sure sign that he is not from God. This is reversed in Paul's case.

General dialogues between Muslims and Christians

Dialogue #1

George (Christian): Salam valeikum!
Ahmad (Muslim): Valeikum assalaam!
George: Is everything ok?
Ahmad: Alhamdulillah (praise be to God)! Yes, everything is ok for me. How about you?
George: Thank God, for me also everything is ok.
Ahmad: I am Ahmad and you…?
George: Hi Ahmad, I am George. Nice meeting you!
Ahmad: Nice meeting you, George. Where are you from?
George: I am from India.
Ahmad: Are you a Muslim?
George: No.
Ahmad: Are you a Hindu?
George: No.
Ahmad: Then what's your religion?
George: Well, I don't believe in religions for they are only human efforts to reach God.
Ahmad: So you are an atheist?
George: No, I believe in God!
Ahmad: Without a religion how do you believe in God?
George: Well, I believe in one God and follow in His truth by following Jesus Christ!
Ahmad: So you are a Christian?

George: If following Jesus Christ and walking in God's truth is to be a Christian, then yes, I am Christian.
Ahmad: Now the final religion is Islam and the final prophet is Muhammad and the final book is Qur'an.
George: Well, that's what Muslims think! In fact, every religion thinks it's the final truth. Even Christians believe that Christianity is the final truth and the Injeel (The New Testament) is the final revelation of God to mankind.
Ahmad: Hmmmm! I see your point. As you said the Injeel was indeed from God, but later it was changed and corrupted and that's why God sent the final book Qur'an.
George: I've read the Injeel and Qur'an. But the Injeel has the best teachings and information about God that I could not find in Qur'an.
Ahmad: Maybe you understood like that, but the current Injeel is not the original Injeel. Because it has been changed and corrupted.
George: Have you read the Injeel?
Ahmad: Uh, yeah!
George: Have you read the Injeel completely?
Ahmad: Oh, no. But some parts.
George: Then how do you know it's changed or corrupted even without reading it fully?
Ahmad: That's a fact, you know...?
George: Really...? If someone comes to you and says, 'I've read only a little bit of Qur'an, but it is a false book don't read it.' What would you think of that person? Do you think he is an intelligent person or unintelligent person?
Ahmad: Of course, such a person is definitely an unintelligent person.
George: That's exactly what I think of you, because that's how you are talking about the Injeel!
Ahmad: ??~!@#$%^&??
George: Sorry if it hurts you, but do you see what you have done by accusing the Injeel, Allah's word, of corruption?
Ahmad: But I am told that Injeel is changed by Christians and that's why Allah had to send the Qur'an to correct it.
George: So you are taught that way! Now I see your problem. Please tell me, according to the Qur'an (S.6:34,115), can anyone change the words of Allah?
Ahmad: No! No one can do that.
George: According to the Qur'an (S.5:43-47), was the Injeel Allah's word when it was sent down or not?
Ahmad: Yes, it was Allah's word.
George: So, according to the Qur'an, Injeel is Allah's word and no one can change Allah's word, but now you are telling me that Injeel is changed and corrupted! Which means Allah's word can be changed by people after all!

The Holy Bible: Muslim Objections and Christian Responses

This means Qur'an is wrong in saying that no one can change Allah's words! Do you see the problem of your wrong opinions about Allah's word?
Ahmad: ……..???.....!!!!!
George: Let me ask you few more questions. If the Injeel were changed, then why would Qur'an tell Christians to follow the Injeel (S.5:47)?
Ahmad: ……?
George: If the Injeel were changed, then why didn't Allah make it plain in the Qur'an saying, 'the Injeel which I sent is corrupted by Christians and therefore don't read it or follow it?'
Ahmad: ……??!!
George: If Injeel were changed and corrupted, then do you have any substantial evidence, other than your wishful thinking, to tell me when it was done, where it was done, how it was done, why it was done and by whom it was done?
Ahmad: …!!!!! Well, it seems that the Injeel you have has variant readings and different versions. That means it is changed?
George: It's true that there are variant readings and different versions of the Injeel. This is because there are thousands of handwritten manuscripts of the Injeel available from even before the Qur'an was given in the early seventh century. Some versions and translations have been made from some sets of manuscript copies and others from other sets of manuscript copies. If the copies have some scribal mistakes because they are made by fallible humans, does that mean the original Injeel is also changed and lost?
Ahmad: I did not understand it properly…?
George: For example, before the advent of printing press, the Qur'an was being produced as hand-written copies by people. During that time if some copyists made some unintentional mistakes in their copies, does that mean the original Qur'an was also affected by those mistakes?
Ahmad: No, how can it be? The mistakes are made and present only in the copies and that too only in some of the copies not necessarily in all of them. That doesn't automatically affect the original Qur'an in anyway.
George: That's exactly what has happened with the copies of the Injeel, too. Most of the ancient Qur'anic copies with variant readings were destroyed during the third Caliph Uthman's time. But the same has not been done in the case of the Injeel. That is why, there are variant readings and different versions. This does not prove that the original Injeel is changed or corrupted or lost.
Ahmad: Oh, my! Now I can see your point, after all.
George: Thanks for understanding my point. May Allah help you to see the truth and not to say any false accusations against Allah's word, the Injeel!

Dialogue # 2

Ahmad: Hi George! How are you today?
George: Salaam Ahmad! I am fine. How about you?
Ahmad: Well, I am also fine, alhamdulilah! I don't have much time today, but still would like to ask you about a small issue in the Bible. Is that ok for you, George?
George: Perfectly alright, for me. What issue you want to talk about?
Ahmad: As I said, I don't have much time to spend with you this time. Please tell me as precisely as possible about the justice of God. I mean when we discuss about God killing people, innocent people, like children, infants and pregnant women, how does your Bible make sense of such actions from God? Is it just for God whom you believe is full of love?
George: Ahmed, definitely this is very important issue. It needs lot of study of the Holy Bible. Since you don't have much time I'll try to put it as short and simple as possible.
Ahmad: That's exactly what I want!
George: Here we go! God is just, but He is also holy. That means God being holy cannot allow any unholy or sinful person to approach and stay in His presence. That's not the end. God is also just. That is why He deals appropriately with either the sin that is committed or the sinner who committed it.
Ahmad: But you said God is also love?!
George: That's correct. But we'll talk more about that and also how God acts in harmony of all these three attributes He has in his nature.
Ahmad: Ok. But tell me now how is it that God who is just can kill innocent people, I mean children?
George: Ahmad, God never acts unjustly. For example, in the case of Sodom and Gomorrah, He destroyed all including, in all probability, children and other innocent people and animals. To put it in a different way, here God poured out His wrath on all as a result of the sin of some!
Ahmad: That's my point!
George: I see that. Please follow me carefully now. There are two important things you need to know and remember in this context.
Ahmad: What are they?
George: One, God's punishment falls on all as a result of the sins of some people. Just like God's blessing falls on all as a result of the righteous deeds of some.
Ahmad: Ok! But still it doesn't look like proper justice.
George: You are right. Until you understand the second point.
Ahmad: What's that?
George: I'm getting there. The punishment God metes out in this world is only temporal. The real punishment will be meted out in the world to come on the Day of Judgment.

Ahmad: That's correct. I know that. But... ?????
George: The innocent such as children, infants and unborn babies who are destroyed or given any share of the punishment of others in this world would be compensated in the world to come according to the justice of God.
Ahmad: That means they won't be punished in the world to come again, right?
George: Precisely! Only those who earn punishment in this world by their evil deeds would receive the eternal punishment on the day of judgment, regardless whether they receive any punishment in this world or not. That way, God still remains just.
Ahmad: This makes sense to me!
George: Well, it should! In fact, even in your Qur'an it is mentioned that Allah has destroyed all people, presumably children, pregnant ladies and animals, in the cities of Sodom and Gomorrah (S. 11:82; 26:169-175; 27:54-58). And also Allah destroyed all except one family in the great flood during Noah's time. No exception for children or pregnant ladies or animals! (S. 26:170-172)
Ahmad: Oh that's true. Now I see your point, and it makes very good sense to me. Thanks, George, for your time and patience with me.
George: Ahmad, you are welcome, my friend.
Ahmad: Let's discuss similar issues next time.
George: No problem. We will do that, Lord willing!
Ahmad: That's correct! Insha Allah! See you later.
George: See you!

The Holy Bible is God's message to mankind—

If you read its pages, you will get knowledge;
If you study its content, you will gain wisdom;
If you love its message, you will be enlightened;
If you embrace its teachings, you will be blessed;
If you walk in its light, you will live forever!

6. SOME EXEGETICAL PRINCIPLES

Unlocking the contents of the Bible requires diligent study and divine help. Many a critic has approached it with wrong intentions and attitudes. They got what they deserved as the Bible forewarned:

"Bear in mind that our Lord's patience means salvation, just as our dear brother Paul also wrote you with the wisdom that God gave him. He writes the same way in all his letters, speaking in them of these matters. His letters contain some things that are hard to understand, <u>which ignorant and unstable people distort, as they do the other Scriptures, to their own destruction.</u> Therefore, dear friends, since you have been forewarned, be on your guard so that you may not be carried away by the error of the lawless and fall from your secure position. But grow in the grace and knowledge of our Lord and Savior Jesus Christ. To him be glory both now and forever! Amen." (2Peter 3:15-18) NIV

For proper understanding and interpretation of the Bible one must follow the principles of the Biblical exegesis. Over and above, God's assistance or illumination is needed to fathom the intended message for individuals as well as communities from the contents of His word. One can receive this assistance when one approaches God's word prayerfully.

The following are some of the exegetical principles that should guide us in our study of the Bible:

1. The Bible is the best interpreter of itself: 'Scripture interprets scripture' is the fundamental principle that must be employed in understanding the Bible. Unlike books produced by mere human authors, the Bible is sufficient for belief, experience, practice and hope. It is also self-sufficient in its authority and authenticity. It neither depends on nor does it need to be supplemented by human traditions.

2. Authority of the Bible: Divine inspiration (Arabic: *ilahi ilham*) is the authority of the Bible. The whole Bible is given under the divine inspiration and as such the entire Bible, in its prescriptive as well as descriptive forms, is the authoritative revelation (Arabic: *wahi*) to mankind from God.

3. Authenticity of the Bible: All the 66 books of the Bible (39 Jewish Scriptures & 27 Christian Scriptures) are divinely inspired books for mankind. Authenticity is related to divine origin, but not to the naming of the human writer(s) or the language employed. Some of the books bear the name of the writer, and some don't. That in itself has no effect upon the authenticity. The following are some of the areas that confirm the Bible's authenticity:

i. Prophetic confirmation
ii. Approval of the prophets and apostles
iii. Unity and agreement among the books
iv. Internal testimony
v. External testimony
vi. Teachings
vii. Transforming power in the lives of the believers

4. Interpretation should begin with explicit statements: The scriptures need to be understood by interpreting implicit statements in the light of explicit statements - not the other way around!

5. Interpretation must follow the context: All Scripture must be interpreted in the light of immediate, greater and whole context of the Bible. The Bible contains many prophecies which form one of the distinctive characteristics of the Bible. Some of the prophecies have more than one fulfilment that need to be interpreted in the whole context of the Bible.

6. Interpretation must be done in the light of the original meanings, genres and times of the Bible: For accurate interpretation the Scriptures in original language need to be consulted. The words and phrases of the Scripture in original language must be understood in their appropriate literary genres and techniques, and also in the cultural and historical contexts of the times that the Scriptures were given.

7. Original message: The original autographs of the 66 books of the Bible were produced by the men of God, either writing themselves or supervising others writing, under the inspiration (*ilahi ilham*) of the Holy Spirit. However, the subsequent copies of the same were done by the scribes who could not be expected to have the same inspiration of the Holy Spirit that was granted to the inspired original writers. This is one of the factors that accounts for the scribal errors and discrepancies found in the numerous copies of the Bible that are available to us that were made in the post-prophetic era. Nevertheless, the sheer number of copies of the Bible that are available to us now ensure that the original message is passed down to us as God intends.

8. Scope of available revelations: God gave revelations (*wahi*) to His holy prophets who spoke and wrote down those revelations for mankind under divine inspiration (*ilahi ilham*). What we have now in our possession is all that we need till the end of the age, but not necessarily all that was inspired in the past!

9. Teachings of the Bible: The Bible is descriptive as well as prescriptive. Descriptive of the past (good & evil) and future (good & evil). Prescriptive of both what is necessary and what is preferable in this world. When the Bible describes past or future evil events or immoral actions that doesn't mean it is promoting or prescribing those events or actions.

10. Three categories of people that understand the Bible: People can be divided into three categories in terms of understanding the true message of the Bible, namely, 'non-believers,' 'believers' and 'inspired men of God.' Non-believers (Nominal Christians, Atheists, Hindus, Muslims etc.) understand the Bible partially and misunderstand it mostly (eg.20% & 80%). Believers (true Christians), who are born again and walk in the light of the biblical teachings, understand the Bible mostly and misunderstand it partially (eg.70% & 30%). But the inspired men of God such as prophets and Apostles understood it fully (100%), except where God restrained them for a purpose (eg.Dan.12:8-10)!

11. Biblical revelations are progressive: The Bible reveals God (His nature, will & plan), man (his purpose, fall & destiny), religion (faith, practice & hope) and salvation (forgiveness, restoration & eternal- life) progressively! For instance, the process of salvation of sinners in the Bible was initially shadowed in the animal sacrifices. However, it is later perfected and established in the sacrificial suffering, death and resurrection of Jesus Christ (Isa al-Masih) who offered Himself willingly for sinful mankind.

12. Biblical phraseology: Since the Bible is originally written in the Hebrew, Aramaic and Greek languages a number of phrases from all these languages have been used in the biblical narratives. 'Sons of God,' 'ancient of days,' 'day of the Lord,' 'seed of the woman,' 'Son of God,' 'son of man,' 'body of Christ,' 'the first-born,' 'light of the world,' 'tree of life' etc. are some of the significant phrases the inspired writers of the Bible used to convey higher spiritual ideas. It is therefore pertinent to consult the original languages and look into the context of a particular phrase and the time when it was employed in order to better understand its intended meaning.

13. Narrative nature of the accounts: The books of the Bible are given in the narrative forms. Different books belong to different genres - prophetic narratives, historic narratives etc. The four gospels of the N.T. are of historic type. Different authors, albeit under the inspiration of God's Spirit, wrote differently about the same events and persons. The details in different accounts might differ, but they never contradict. The information they provide and the incidents they highlight were largely intended to help their primary audience in their respective contexts.

14. God is in charge of His books: The Almighty God is the giver, protector and fulfiller of the Scriptures He gave to mankind. None, man or devil, is able to make God fail in these areas! Only an unbeliever disputes this truth. In the light of this truth, we can affirm that the original message of God is still fully in-tact either in the form of one of the numerous copies we now have or spread around all the available copies that we have today.

But, in these last days the enemy of God has been trying in many ways to cast doubt in the minds and hearts of people, as in the case of Adam and Eve's fall, about God's word. One of the shameful lies of Satan is, 'The Bible is changed or corrupted and therefore it is not reliable!' Unfortunately, many gullible people who do not believe in God's power to protect His word have fallen prey to this lie of the evil one.

May the One true God lead you and guide you into all truth as you read and study His word the Holy Bible!

Website: http://www.christiansanswermuslims.org/

This book is also available in Kindle edition

BIBLIOGRAPHY

1. Norman L. Geisler, *Christian Apologetics*, Baker Book House, 1976
2. Foud Elias Accad, *Building Bridges*, Navpress, 1997
3. James R. White, *What Every Christian Needs to Know About The Qur'an*, Bethany House Publishers, 2013
4. David Goldman, *Islam and the Bible*, Moody Publishers, Chicago, 2004
5. Norman L. Geisler and Abdul Saleeb, *Answering Islam*, Baker Books, 1993
6. Edward J. Hoskins, *A Muslim's Heart*, Navpress, 2005
7. Samuel Green, *Different Arabic Versions of the Qur'an*, online article at http://www.answering-islam.org/Green/seven.htm
8. Steven Masood, *More than conquerors*, Paternoster Publishing, 2001
9. Phil Parshall, *The Cross and The Crescent*, Gabriel Publications, 2002
10. Samuel Green, *The Preservation of Qur'an*, the online article at http://engagingwithislam.org/leaflets/Preservation_Qur'an.pdf
11. Brother Mark, *A 'Perfect Qur'an' or 'So it was made to appear to them'?*
12. Ahmed Deedat, *Christ in Islam*, Golden Empire Publications, 2011
13. Ali Dashti, *Twenty Three Years: A study of the prophetic career of Muhammad*, Mazda Publications, 1994
14. Rashad Khalifa, *Qur'an, Hadith and Islam*, Universal Unity, 2000
15. Islamic Website on Qur'an MSS, *Islamic Awareness.org*, http://www.islamic-awareness.org/Qur'an/Text/Mss/
16. Jay Smith, *An Historic Critique of Islam's Beginnings*, Online Presentation at https://www.youtube.com/watch?v=Zd9lIuUjPs0

Printed in Great Britain
by Amazon